Arkansas & Missouri Railroad: History Through the Miles

by Barton Jennings

Arkansas & Missouri Railroad: History Through the Miles
Copyright © 2016 by Barton Jennings

All rights reserved. This book may not be duplicated or transmitted in any way, or stored in an information retrieval system, without the express written consent of the publisher, except in the form of brief excerpts or quotations for the purpose of review. Making copies of this book, or any portion, for any purpose other than your own, is a violation of United States copyright laws.

Publisher's Cataloging-in-Publication Data
Jennings, Barton

Arkansas & Missouri Railroad: History Through the Miles
136p.; 21cm.
ISBN: 978-0-9849866-5-1

Library of Congress Control Number: 2016904253

First Edition
135798642

Front cover photo by Gregory Molloy
Back cover photo by Sarah Jennings

TechScribes, Inc.
PO Box 620
Avon, IL 61415
www.techscribes.com

Printed in the United States of America

Contents

Arkansas & Missouri Railroad 5
Freight Trains 7
Passenger Trains and Cars 9
Locomotives 12
Radio Frequencies 18
Welcome to the Northwest Arkansas Region 19
A Bit About the Country 20
A Bit About the History 22
A Bit About Today 24
An Introduction to Springdale, Arkansas 27
History of the Route of the Arkansas & Missouri Railroad: The St. Louis and San Francisco Railway Company 31
Frisco Passenger Trains 34
Route Guides 37
Route Guide: Springdale to Van Buren 39
The Rest of the Railroad 81
Route Guide: Monett to Sprindgale 83
Route Guide: Bentonville Branch 111
Route Guide: Van Buren to South Fort Smith 115
Glossary 133
About the Author and Book 135

Arkansas & Missouri Railroad: History Through the Miles

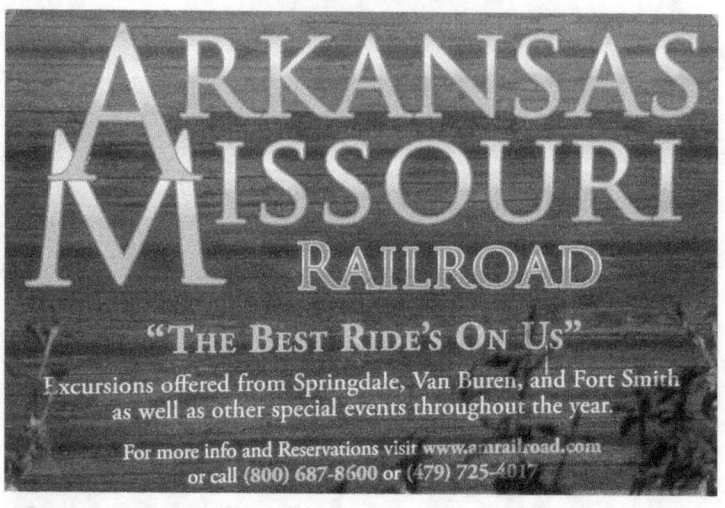

Photos by Barton Jennings.

Arkansas & Missouri Railroad

The Arkansas & Missouri may be one of the most documented shortline railroads in the country. Articles on it, and its large fleet of Alco locomotives, have been published in many magazines such as *Trains*, *Railfan & Railroad*, and *Pacific Rail News*. Finding information on the railroad is little challenge for the serious railfan.

The A&M was founded in 1985 by an investor group, headed up by Tony Hannold (operator of several shortline railroads on the east coast), which signed a lease-purchase agreement with Burlington Northern (BN) for this line. At the time, northwest Arkansas was considered to be a poor part of the country and BN was centering their investment efforts on their mainlines. However, since the creation of the line, this region has become one of the most dynamic business centers in the United States. Companies such as Tyson Foods, Walmart, and J.B. Hunt are headquartered along the line.

At the time of the purchase, the principal items hauled consisted of timber products, canned goods, chicken feed, sand and gravel. Today, the traffic mix has somewhat changed with more than 150 shippers using the railroad. Probably the most visible shipments are the significant inbound quantities of grain and grain products as feed for industry giants Tyson Foods, George's, Cargill, OK Feeds, and Willowbrook Foods. The A&M also moves large volumes of frozen poultry for Frez-N-Stor, Zero Mountain, OK Foods Industries, and Arkansas Refrigerated, as well as canned vegetables for Allen Canning. The railroad also delivers the ingredients for Newly Weds Foods (batters, breadings, and seasoning systems), Pepper Source (tangy, spicy sauces), and Pappas Foods (juices and syrups), as well as materials for Glad (manufactures storage bags and plastic wrappings), Smurfit-Stone Container, and Georgia-Pacific (cups and containers).

The A&M also operates regular shipments of sand for major concrete producers Arkhola Sand and Gravel, Mid-Continent Concrete, Beaver Lake Concrete, Tune Concrete, Kay Concrete, and Barry County Ready Mix, among others. Cement is handled for Ash Grove Cement, and timber is moved for National Home

Centers, Ridout Lumber, Meeks Lumber, and Midwest Walnut. Scrap steel is moved for Davis Iron and Metal, Rogers Iron and Metal, and Roll Off Services; pellets go to St. Gobain Proppants; and plastic materials to Van Buren Pipe.

The railroad interchanges with BNSF at Monett, Union Pacific at Van Buren, and Kansas City Southern at Fort Smith. Additionally, the A&M handles direct barge-rail shipments at the Arkansas River ports of Van Buren and Fort Smith. The Arkansas & Missouri has also created an affiliate, Ozark Transmodal, Inc., to handle transload freight movements.

In 2000, the railroad leased 3.2 miles of track (locally known as "the Bottoms") from Union Pacific at Van Buren to reach a sand barge dock, and provides haulage services for Union Pacific between Van Buren and the Fort Smith Railroad in Fort Smith.

On March 16, 2001, the Arkansas & Missouri Railroad actually purchased the Monett to Fort Smith line. In June 2002, Tony Hannold was replaced as chairman of the railroad by Reilly McCarren, former president and chief executive officer of the Wisconsin Central Transportation Corporation. McCarren also soon became the majority stockholder of the railroad. During the next three years, the new ownership essentially rebuilt the railroad, adding welded rail where lighter jointed rail existed south of Springdale.

During the past decade, the railroad has continued to modernize with a new office, passenger station, and locomotive and car shop. The Alco fleet continued to expand until the availability of quality locomotives, and the increase in freight, required larger and more modern locomotives. In 2013, Electro-Motive Diesel (EMD) delivered three SD70ACes locomotives to the A&M. The locomotives were the three demonstrators that have been seen across the country, numbered 1201-1203. EMD 1201 was particularly famous as it was the EMD demonstrator painted in Caterpillar colors that was unveiled at Caterpillar's exhibit at MINExpo in 2012.

Arkansas & Missouri Railroad

Photo by Barton Jennings.

Freight Trains

The A&M is essentially a 24-hours a day, seven days a week freight operator. Local trains operate out of both the Springdale and Fort Smith terminals, serving more than 150 freight customers. Customers are centered at the two major terminals and freight is interchanged at Monett with BNSF, at Van Buren with Union Pacific, and with Kansas City Southern in Fort Smith. The A&M also handles UP freight being moved from Van Buren to the Fort Smith Railroad's yard in Fort Smith.

When the Arkansas & Missouri Railroad started up, the pattern was to have a daytime run down to Fort Smith and back, with a run to the BN at Monett at night. These two trains used the same basic consist of C-420 Alco locomotives. Servicing was done between the runs and by swapping a few of the locomotives on a daily basis since the trains generally only took three or four locomotives. Local trains at Springdale used the extra C-420 locomotives not needed on the Turns, while local trains at Fort Smith used the fleet of T-6 locomotives

Over the years, this pattern has changed greatly. First, a few years ago the routing of the Turns were reversed, with the Monett Turn becoming the daytime train and the Fort Smith Turn leaving about 10pm and returning to Springdale soon after daylight the next morning. A second major change was the number of locomotives required to haul the trains. Seeing as many as seven C-420s on a single Fort Smith Turn is an impressive sunrise scene on today's Arkansas & Missouri. In the Fort Smith area, a single T-6 is no longer powerful enough for most trains, and it is not uncommon to see several C-420 or other locomotives assigned to these locals. Locals in the Springdale area also use the newest of Alco power to handle the freight volumes.

With the arrival of the new SD70ACes locomotives in 2013, the Monett and Fort Smith Turns now typically are powered by the newer locomotives, with the heavier Alco power being used on the locals. Some locomotives have also been leased to other operations across the region.

In Springdale, North Yard is the center of train activity. Freights are built and torn down here, and locals pick up their cars and return them here. Locals generally work the Rogers area, Springdale, and Fayetteville, meaning that several locals are on the road daily. In Fort Smith, there are generally two locals operating with one handling local business and the other handling UP interchange movements and the larger customers. These locals are based in the former Frisco Yard just north of downtown.

An additional change on the railroad is the presence of Union Pacific shuttle grain trains. On January 14, 2006, the first UP shuttle on the A&M delivered 73 cars of corn for poultry feed mills on the railroad. The new connection at Van Buren was designed to make this move more efficient. Before the use of these shuttle trains, approximately 50 percent of the grain arrived by truck; the shuttle trains have grabbed much of this market. Recently, similar grain trains have arrived via BNSF.

The line handles 286,000 pound railcars (the railroad industry standard) and has vertical clearances sufficient for double-stack intermodal cars. The movement of high-wide specials across the railroad is not an uncommon event.

Arkansas & Missouri Railroad

Photo by Barton Jennings.

Passenger Trains and Cars

Passenger service began on the Arkansas & Missouri Railroad during the late 1980s and went full time during the early 1990s after a private operator tested the market and operated passenger trains for a year. Over the years, the route and equipment have changed a bit, but they have always focused on the scenery and history of the region.

Today, the A&M operates a series of regular passenger trains throughout the year. Approximately 40,000 people a year ride these trains. The normal schedule includes a Springdale to Van Buren round-trip, with a Van Buren to Winslow round-trip during the layover. However, other trips are operated including short Santa trains and trains for special community events. Seating is available in restored commuter coaches, a parlor car, a dining car, and even a rare dome car.

Coach #104 "*Biloxi Blues*" was used in the Neil Simon movie of the same name. The filming was done at Fort Chaffee, Van Buren, and on the Arkansas & Missouri Railroad. The car, built for the Delaware, Lackawanna & Western's steam powered suburban service out of Hoboken, New Jersey, reportedly carried commuters in New Jersey until 1982. The car was built by

Pullman in 1917 as an early steel car using many of the design standards used with earlier wooden cars. It has open end platforms (one of the last large orders of open-platform coaches ever built), windows that open, and clerestory roofs. The car seats 72 passengers and has no air conditioning.

Coach #105 "*Golden Age*" was built by Harlan & Hollingsworth (Bethlehem Steel) in 1927 for the Central Railroad of New Jersey. Harlan & Hollingsworth was a Wilmington, Delaware, firm that constructed ships and railroad cars. It was acquired by Bethlehem Steel during December 1904. The shipyard closed in 1926. However, railcars were built on the site until 1940, and parts for railroad cars until 1944. The car served in commuter service for many years, and has closed vestibules. The Central Railroad of New Jersey ran this and similar cars out of their Jersey City terminal where commuters caught ferries on to New York. This terminal is now used by the ferries to the Statue of Liberty and the Ellis Island Immigration Station. The car has 72 passenger seats as well as a conductor's cabin. Coach #105 is air conditioned.

Coach #106 "*Mountain View*" is a sister to coach #105 with a similar history. It also seats 72 passengers plus two more seats next to the restroom. It too has air conditioning.

Parlor Car #107 "*Explorer*" was built by Pullman Standard in 1955-1956 as Long Island Railroad class P72 coach 2927. The car was rebuilt in 1989 by the LIRR as class PP72B parlor car 2002. This car was one of only two "dual mode" parlor cars, capable of drawing power from either its installed diesel generator system or from a trainline. When the car was retired, it was acquired by Ken Bitten and used as a table car on the Northern Central Railway in Pennsylvania. After the Northern Central shut down, the car moved to the Arkansas & Missouri Railroad in December 2004. This car also has an open platform.

Dome #108 "*Silver Feather*" started life as Western Pacific dome coach #812 "*Silver Feather*," built by Budd in 1948 for the famous California Zephyr. Today, the car has table seating in the dome and vestibule end because of its later use in a dinner train. When retired, the car went to the Auto Train where it was painted and renumbered as #461. By the mid-1980s, the car was restored to its California Zephyr look and name and served on the Texas Southern operation. The car then became Washington Central (WCRC) #151 in 1993 before moving to BC Rail and their Pacific Starlight Dinner Train in 1997. There, the car retained the 151 number, but acquired the name "*Moonglow*." With changes on the railroad, the operation was shut down and the car listed for sale by late 2002. In February 2004, the car was sold to the Ontario Northland and renumbered 901. The car was again sold in December, 2010, and arrived on the Arkansas & Missouri by late 2011, where it was numbered 108 and renamed "*Silver Feather.*"

Diner-Lounge #109 "*Spirit of Arkansas*" entered service on August 20, 1950, as a Southern Pacific Sunset Limited "Pride of Texas" coffee shop-lounge car. Numbered SP 10409, the car was decorated with Texas cattle brands and featured inexpensive meals for coach passengers. Known by some as a hamburger grill car, the car was built by Budd with 32 dining table seats, 14 lounge-table seats, a bar and a kitchen. The car became Amtrak 8322 in 1971. After being retired, the car became owned by Hank Peterson (RPCX 8322) and used on trips on the Ohio Central. The A&M acquired the car in early 2014.

Photo by Barton Jennings.

Photo by Barton Jennings.

Locomotives

The Arkansas & Missouri Railroad has long been known as a haven for locomotives built by the American Locomotive Company (Alco). Historically, leading many of the freights is a C-420, probably the best of the mid-horsepower locomotives that Alco manufactured during its last days. Actually, EMD power was initially used by the A&M, but the available locomotives proved to be slippery on the steep grades and Alco power was tried with good success. All of the Alco and Montreal Locomotive Works locomotives are second hand, and they have come from many railroads across the country. Recently, new Electro-Motive Diesel (EMD) power has returned on the mainline runs of the Arkansas & Missouri Railroad.

The following information includes the model, build date, manufacturer and serial number, and ownership history of the railroad's locomotive fleet. It should be noted that many of these locomotives are not on the railroad, but are instead leased to industries across the region. Additionally, there have been a num-

Arkansas & Missouri Railroad

ber of locomotives credited to the Arkansas & Missouri Railroad which were actually owned by DMV, a locomotive leasing company operated by Tony Hannold. These locomotives would often be seen on the property of the A&M, but many were here only until sold.

Engine #	Model	Bld Date	Mfr/Const #	Notes
12	T-6	10/59	Alco 83388	Built as Norfolk & Western 46, to Maryland & Delaware 12, to Arkansas & Missouri 12
14	T-6	9/59	Alco 83385	Built as Norfolk & Western 43, to Maryland & Delaware 14, to Arkansas & Missouri 14
15	T-6	3/58	Alco 82862	Built as Pennsylvania 8429, to Penn Central 9849, to Conrail 9849, to North Country RR 100, to Maryland & Delaware 15, to Avtex Fibers 415, to Arkansas & Missouri 15
16	T-6	7/59	Alco 83376	Built as Norfolk & Western 34, to Maryland & Delaware 16, to Arkansas & Missouri 16
17	T-6	3/58	Alco 82857	Built as Pennsylvania 8424, to Penn Central 9844, to Conrail 9844, to Maryland & Delaware 17, to Eastern Shore 17, to Delaware Coast Line 17, to Arkansas & Missouri 17
18	T-6	3/59	Alco 82320	Built as Norfolk & Western 19, to Maryland & Delaware 18, to Arkansas & Missouri 18
20	RS-1	10/51	Alco 79349	Built as Rutland 400, to Tennessee RR 4, to Southern 4, to Public Utilities Commission-South Carolina 4, to Virginia & Maryland 20, to Maryland & Delaware 20, to Arkansas & Missouri 20
22	RS-1	4/43	Alco 70811	Built as Atlanta & St. Andrews Bay 905, to Tennessee RR 1, to Southern 1, to Public Utilities Commission-South Carolina 1, to Maryland & Delaware 22, to Arkansas & Missouri 22, retired and to Museum of Transportation (St. Louis)

30	RS-32	6/61	Alco 83992	Built as New York Central 8031, to Penn Central 2031, to Conrail 2031, to Maryland & Delaware 42, to Arkansas & Missouri 42, renumbered 30
32	C-424	4/65	Alco 3382-06	Built as Belt Railroad of Chicago 601, to Arkansas & Missouri 01, renumbered 32
34	C-424	4/65	Alco 3382-07	Built as Belt Railroad of Chicago 602, to Arkansas & Missouri 02, renumbered 34
40	C-420	8/67	Alco 3490-09	Built as Monon 515, to Louisville & Nashville 1332, to Chrome Crankshaft 332, to Indiana Hi-Rail 332, to Wabash and Ohio 332, to Indiana Box Car Corporation 332, to Arkansas & Missouri 40
42	C-420	2/65	Alco 3437-01	Built as Erie Mining 600, to Ohio Central 7220, to Arkansas & Missouri 42
44	C-420	6/65	Alco 3418-03	Built as Seaboard Air Line 112, to Seaboard Coast Line 1214, to Louisville & Nashville 1353, to Arkansas & Missouri 44
46	C-420	6/65	Alco 3418-04	Built as Seaboard Air Line 113, to Seaboard Coast Line 1215, to Louisville & Nashville 1354, to Arkansas & Missouri 46
48	C-420	8/65	Alco 3418-16	Built as Seaboard Air Line 125, to Seaboard Coast Line 1227, to Louisville & Nashville 1366, to Arkansas & Missouri 48
50	C-420	3/63	Alco 84721	Built as Lehigh & Hudson River 22, to Essex Terminal 106, to Arkansas & Missouri 50
52	C-420	1/66	Alco 3431-01	Built as Lehigh & Hudson River 23, to Conrail 2073, to Maryland & Delaware 52, to Arkansas & Missouri 52
54	C-420	1/66	Alco 3431-02	Built as Lehigh & Hudson River 24, to Conrail 2074, to Maryland & Delaware 54, to Arkansas & Missouri 54
56	C-420	1/66	Alco 3431-03	Built as Lehigh & Hudson River 25, to BC Rail 631, to Arkansas & Missouri 56

Arkansas & Missouri Railroad

57	C-420	1/66	Alco 3431-04	Built as Lehigh & Hudson River 26, to BC Rail 632, to Arkansas & Missouri 57
58	C-420	7/66	Alco 3463-03	Built as Lehigh & Hudson River 29, to Conrail 2077, to Delaware & Hudson 401, renumbered 420, to Arkansas & Missouri 58
60	C-420	10/64	Alco 3385-10	Built as Lehigh Valley 413, to Delaware & Hudson 413, to Arkansas & Missouri 60
62:1	GP40	9/68	EMD 34342	Built as Penn Central 3165, to Conrail 3165, to Arkansas & Missouri 62, to Kyle 3112, to Helm Leasing 3112, rebuilt, to Dakota, Minnesota & Eastern 3835, to Arkansas & Missouri 62
62:2	C-420	10/64	Alco 3385-03	Built as Lehigh Valley 406, to Delaware & Hudson 406, renumbered 416, to Arkansas & Missouri 62
63	C-420	9/65	Alco 3425-01	Built as Mississippi Export 63, to MPCO 63, to Arkansas & Missouri 63
64	C-420	10/64	Alco 3385-04	Built as Lehigh Valley 407, to Delaware & Hudson 407, renumbered 417, to Arkansas & Missouri 64
66	C-420	10/64	Alco 3385-09	Built as Lehigh Valley 412, to Delaware & Hudson 412, to Arkansas & Missouri 66
68	C-420	10/64	Alco 3385-08	Built as Lehigh Valley 411, to Delaware & Hudson 411, to Arkansas & Missouri 411, to Indiana Hi-Rail 311, to Arkansas & Missouri 68
70:1	C-630	7/68	MLW 6002-01	Built as Canadian Pacific 4500, to Western New York & Pennsylvania 630, to Arkansas & Missouri 70
70:2	M-420	6/74	MLW 6081-24	Built as Canadian National 3553, to Ohio Central 3553, to Arkansas & Missouri 70
70:3	SD70ACe	5/2012	EMD 20116604A-005	Built as EMDX 1201, CAT display locomotive, to Arkansas & Missouri 70

71	SD70ACe	5/2012	EMD 20116604A-001 Built as EMDX 2110, renumbered 1202, EMD Demonstrator, to Arkansas & Missouri 71
72:1	M-420	6/74	MLW 6081-25 Built as Canadian National 3554, to Ohio Central 3554, to Arkansas & Missouri 72
72:2	SD70ACe	5/2012	EMD 20116604A-002 Built as EMDX 2111, renumbered 1203, EMD Demonstrator, to Arkansas & Missouri 72
74	M-420	10/76	MLW 6092-08 Built as Canadian National 2567, renumbered 3567, to Ohio Central 3567, to Arkansas & Missouri 74
76	HR412	10/81	MLW 6115-09 Built as Canadian National 2588, renumbered 3588, to Ohio Central 3588, to Arkansas & Missouri 76
80	TEBU	34704	Built as Southern Pacific U25B 6712, rebuilt by Morrison Knudsen to TEBU, to Southern Pacific 1606, to MJRX 1606, to Arkansas & Missouri 80
600	C-424	4/65	Alco 3382-05 Built as Belt Railroad of Chicago 600, to Hudson Bay 600, to Arkansas & Missouri for parts
604	C-424	5/66	Alco 3450-02 Built as Belt Railroad of Chicago 604, to Hudson Bay 604, to Arkansas & Missouri for parts
605	C-424	5/66	Alco 3450-03 Built as Belt Railroad of Chicago 605, to Hudson Bay 605, to VLIX 605, to Arkansas & Missouri for parts
4222	C-424	10/65	MLW 84860 Built as Canadian Pacific 8322, renumbered 4222, to Quebec Central 4222, to Louisville, New Albany and Corydon 4222, to Arkansas & Missouri 4222
4242	C-424	1/66	MLW 3436-10 Built as Canadian Pacific 4242, to Quebec Central 4242, to Louisville, New Albany and Corydon 4242, to Arkansas & Missouri 4242

Arkansas & Missouri Railroad

Photos by Barton Jennings.

Radio Frequencies

The Arkansas & Missouri Railroad uses a number of radio frequencies, especially when interchanging with its many neighboring railroads. For those wanting to listen in, here are the frequencies assigned to the railroad. The AAR reference is for the Association of American Railroads, the organization which manages the radio frequencies for the United States railroad industry.

160.440 AAR Channel 22 A&M Channel 1	Road Channel
160.785 AAR Channel 45 A&M Channel 2	Yard Channel
161.160 AAR Channel 70 A&M Channel 3	BNSF Interchange at Monnett, MO
161.475 AAR Channel 91	A&M Channel 4 Maintenance of Way

The Arkansas & Missouri Railroad website at **www.amrailroad.com** has information about the railroad and its regular freight and passenger services.

Welcome to the Northwest Arkansas Region

This part of the United States is one of the most prosperous in the country. Driven by the success of local companies like Walmart, Tyson Foods, and J.B. Hunt, thousands of other companies have located nearby. For example, most Fortune 500 manufacturers have representatives in the region. The quad cities of Fayetteville, Springdale, Rogers and Bentonville, as well as Lowell, Johnson, West Fork, and other smaller towns in the region, have all boomed, changing from quiet rural communities to a large metropolitan network of industries, subdivisions and shopping malls. For example, during the 1990s, more than 2,000 people a month moved to the region and the unemployment rate is typically half of the national average.

According to the *2012 State of the Northwest Arkansas Region Report*, "The Northwest Arkansas region is defined as the Fayetteville-Springdale-Rogers metropolitan statistical area, which is comprised of Benton, Madison, and Washington counties in Arkansas and McDonald County in Missouri. The region includes 50 incorporated cities and 15 unincorporated communities. According to 2011 U.S. Census estimates, the population of the Northwest Arkansas region was 473,830 and grew at a rate of 1.7 percent between 2010 and 2011."

Nevertheless, the region is still blessed with miles of heavy woods and countryside. Much of the area still has few if any roads and only local farms dot the hillside. Most of the towns on the area railroads have populations of less than a thousand, with many residents commuting to the larger cities for jobs. However, industry does exist with poultry plants, feedmills, and many other potential rail shippers across the area. Tourism is a major business for the area with its many state parks, lakes, and historic attractions.

A Bit About the Country

Arkansas can be a confusing state for many people, depending upon which part they visit. For many people, it is a mountainous state, for others, it's part of the Mississippi River delta. Both are right as Arkansas can be split into two parts – the highlands in the northwest and the lowlands of the southeast. Northwest Arkansas is part of the Ozark Plateau, which includes the Ozark Mountains. Divided by the Arkansas River, to the south of Fort Smith are the Ouachita Mountains. These two mountain ranges are part of the Interior Highlands region, the only major mountainous region between the Rocky Mountains and the Appalachian Mountains.

Arkansas summers can be hot and wet, with a June average high temperature of 84 degrees in Fayetteville, with an average low of 64 degrees. Fort Smith is normally about 3 degrees warmer. Arkansas' all-time record high is 120°F at Ozark on August 10, 1936, and the all-time record low is -29°F at Gravette on February 13, 1905. Rainfall averages 40 to 60 inches a year, with June often featuring three inches or more, often from short but strong thunderstorms.

As you travel through the woods of northwest Arkansas and southwest Missouri, it should be pointed out that trees are a recent addition to a large part of the region. Until the 20th Century, much of the area along the railroad was primarily prairie, kept down by the herds of bison and elk, and later farmers and their crops. Only small areas of original prairie still exist in the region, although efforts are under way to restore more prairie lands. Two early reports explain what it was like in the early 1800s.

Henry Rowe Schoolcraft and Levi Pettibone explored the area from November 1818 to February 1819, covering the area from Missouri to the White River and Osage Creek regions of northwest Arkansas. They surveyed the geography, geology, and mineralogy of the area. A report of the trip was published by Schoolcraft in 1821 entitled *Journal of a Tour into the Interior of Missouri and Arkansaw*. This was the first written account of an exploration of the Ozarks and tallgrass prairies of northwest Arkansas.

In the report, Schoolcraft wrote, "Our route this day has been over barrens and prairies, with occasional forests of oak, the soil poor, and covered with grass, with very little under-brush. One of the greatest inconveniences we experience in travelling in this region, arises from the difficulty of finding, at the proper time, a place of encampment affording wood and water, both of which are indispensable. This is a difficulty which attends us this evening, having been compelled to stop in an open prairie, where wood is very scarce, and the water bad-general course of traveling south-weather pleasant, the rain having ceased shortly after day-light. Lands poor; trees, oaks; game observed; deer and elk."

Schoolcraft continued: "In calling this a high-land prairie, I am to be understood as meaning a tract of high-land generally level, and with very little wood or shrubbery. It is a level woodless barren covered with wild grass, and resembling the natural meadows or prairies of the western country in appearance. The inducements for hunting are, however, great; and large quantities of bear, deer, elk, and beaver skins, might be collected."

"The prairies, which commence at the distance of a mile west of this river, are the most extensive, rich, and beautiful, of any which I have ever seen west of the Mississippi river. They are covered by a coarse wild grass, which attains so great a height that it completely hides a man on horseback in riding through it. The deer and elk abound in this quarter, and the buffaloe is occasionally seen in droves upon the prairies, and in the open high-land woods."

Also in 1819, naturalist Thomas Nuttall journeyed through the Arkansas Territory and documented a "vast and trackless wilderness of trees" and "great prairies and canebrakes". Nuttall reported bison, eastern elk, swans, passenger pigeons, ruffed grouse, and prairie chickens among the abundant wildlife populations that made their homes in the Arkansas Territory during this time.

Not long thereafter, however, as the territory became settled, species began to disappear. Less than a century after Nuttall's journey through Arkansas, little remained of the virgin upland and bottomland forests and tall grass prairies. The eastern elk lived in eastern hardwood forests and prairies, and were native to northwest Arkansas. Historical accounts indicate elk were the first game species to be killed out, having vanished from the region by the 1840s, and becoming extinct soon thereafter. American bison herds were common to northwest Arkansas tall grass prairies. By 1870, none were left in Arkansas. Packs of gray wolves that often followed bison herds were exterminated from Arkansas after the beginning of the 20th century, and the red wolf disappeared by 1950. Today, many animals such as bear, deer, elk, and many game birds are back. Many are often seen from the train.

There's an old folk saying about the Ozarks: "It's not that the mountains are so high, it's just that the valleys are so deep." It's true. The Ozarks are a heavily eroded plateau, pushed up eons ago and carved out by hundreds of streams over thousands of years. Even the highest Ozark mountains barely exceed 2,000 feet in elevation, but they are certainly rugged with the numerous streams eating out valleys. Enjoy the views.

A Bit About the History

Until Europeans arrived, Arkansas was inhabited by the Caddo, Osage, and Quapaw tribes. The first European explorer to visit Arkansas was Hernando de Soto in 1541. Jacques Marquette and Louis Jolliet followed in 1673. The first European settlement was at Arkansas Post (founded in 1686), originally a Quapaw village in eastern Arkansas on the Arkansas River. The name Arkansas actually comes from the Illinois tribe's name for the Quapaw people. The only American Revolutionary War battle fought in Arkansas happened at Arkansas Post during April 1783. After the Louisiana Purchase, Arkansas was briefly a part of the Missouri Territory before becoming the Arkansas Territory, including lands in Oklahoma. The Territory of Arkansas was admitted to the Union as the 25th state on June 15, 1836.

Northwest Arkansas and southwest Missouri have been the site of many historic activities throughout the history of the United States. Early Spanish explorers crossed this region in the

Welcome to the Northwest Arkansas Region

1500s looking for land and wealth. The French explored the edges of the region during the 1700s, primarily sticking to the surrounding waterways. However, with the acquisition of the land by the United States as a part of the 1803 Louisiana Purchase, more detailed exploration and settlement of the land began.

The Trail of Tears focused heavily upon northwest Arkansas. The Trail, a name describing the forced relocation of various Native American nations from southeastern parts of the United States, was actually a series of routes used following the Indian Removal Act of 1830. In 1831, the Choctaw were the first to be removed, with the Seminole removed in 1832, the Creek in 1834, the Chickasaw in 1837, and finally the Cherokee in 1838. The various tribes were moved using different routes, including a water route up the Arkansas River through Fort Smith, a land route from Memphis to Little Rock and then west along the river through Van Buren (Bell-Drane Route), a land route across the rugged Ozarks through Fayetteville (Benge Route), and a land route across Missouri through Springfield (MO) and along the route of the Arkansas & Missouri Railroad to Fayetteville and then west (Northern Route).

The Civil War also heavily impacted this region. The largest battle west of the Mississippi River was fought at Pea Ridge (Elkhorn Tavern) on March 7-8, 1862. 26,000 soldiers fought just a few miles north of Rogers to decide the fate of Missouri and the West, and most of the battlefield is preserved as a National Military Park. Later that year on December 7, 1862, the Battle of Prairie Grove (southwest of Fayetteville) effectively removed northwest Arkansas as a route for Confederate troops to use to invade Missouri. The rest of the war primarily saw guerrilla activity and numerous battles between small units moving throughout the mountains. In fact, few towns in the area escaped being burned at least once.

Once peace returned, this mountainous area was settled mostly by farmers from similar mountainous areas to the east such as Tennessee and Pennsylvania. At one time or another, most of this area was planted in cotton and corn, but the thin soil didn't last long, and much of the land was essentially abandoned to forests. The forests in the more rugged areas were soon logged, leading to further erosion. During the 1940s through the 1960s, a series of dams were built on area rivers. Today, this combination of events has led to the area becoming a major vacation area as a combination of numerous lakes and parks attracts millions each year.

A Bit About Today

For those trying to understand the geography of the area, Interstate 49 runs north from Fort Smith (Arkansas' second largest city with a population of 90,000) to just north of Bentonville near the Arkansas-Missouri border. This seventy-five mile long highway basically parallels the Arkansas & Missouri Railroad, often crossing the railroad on towering bridges connecting ridge top to ridge top. The southern forty miles of the highway passes through a few rural communities, but basically dances along Ozark mountain tops. Once at Fayetteville, the Interstate passes through town after town, creating a narrow city. From south to north, the towns are Fayetteville, Springdale, Lowell, Rogers, Bentonville, and Bella Vista.

Fayetteville, the state's third largest city with a population of 80,000, is the home of the University of Arkansas and until recently considered to be the "Capitol of Northwest Arkansas." Just to its north, Springdale is the state's fourth-largest city at more than 75,000. Tyson Foods, the world's largest producer of protein, has its headquarters here, as well as the Northwest Arkansas Naturals – the Double A affiliate of the Kansas City Royals baseball team. Next is Lowell, home of J.B. Hunt Transport Services, Inc., one of the largest transportation logistics companies in North America, and one of the first domestic trucking companies to move major parts of their business to rail intermodal.

Just north of Lowell is Rogers, population of 60,000 and home of Daisy Manufacturing Company since 1958. The Rogers Daisy Airgun Museum is located in downtown Rogers and is home to the world's largest collection of antique airguns, BB guns and commemorative rifles. Bentonville, the home of Walmart, is next. What until just a few years ago was a small mountain community is now the home of 40,000 and almost as

Welcome to the Northwest Arkansas Region

many different corporate offices as New York City. Just south of the Missouri state line is Bella Vista, a community of 25,000 that primarily serves as an affluent retirement community.

About thirty minutes west of this line is Oklahoma, and the western edge of the Ozarks. This area becomes drier and more prairie-like as you go west. Heading south, the Arkansas River valley passes between Van Buren and Fort Smith, with the Ouachita Mountains a bit farther south. Fort Smith, because of its location in the valley, is often the hottest city in Arkansas. Heading east, the Ozark Mountains get more rugged as numerous streams have cut down into the Ozark Plateau. Beaver Lake is here, the uppermost major dam and lake on the White River. Heading north, the country becomes more rolling as the Plateau becomes more pronounced and you enter Missouri.

The Ozark Plateau of Northwest Arkansas. Photo by Sarah Jennings.

Photo by Barton Jennings.

An Introduction to Springdale, Arkansas

According to several sources on the history of northwest Arkansas, people have lived in the area now called Springdale for about 12,000 years. Early settlers came and stayed because of abundant natural resources, just as later European settlers did. Osage Indians from farther north used the area for seasonal hunting in the late eighteenth and early nineteenth centuries. The Cherokee Treaty of 1828 allowed white settlers to lay claim to the area, and families from eastern states began settling here.

A spring in this area attracted both humans and animals. A community here started in 1838, and in 1839, John Fitzgerald and his wife, Mary, built an inn called Fitzgerald's Station near the spring. When the last of the native tribes of the east were moved to the Oklahoma area, the inn became a stop for those on the Trail of Tears. In 1843, the Shiloh Primitive Baptist Church was built on property donated by William Davidson Quinton and located near the spring. In 1858, the Butterfield Overland Mail route was located through what would become Springdale, and Fitzgerald's Station became an official station.

As the town grew, land speculators soon followed. One of these, John Holcombe, is considered to be the founder of the town that grew around the spring and small church. Though not an original settler, Holcombe was a charismatic man who understood that it was wise to buy land and organize a town. He was responsible for laying out the town plats on land he acquired and giving plots to business people so the town would prosper. Referred to as Holcombe Springs for a time, the church and settlement soon became known as Shiloh after the church.

While the next decade or so saw the community grow, the Civil War wasn't kind to the area. Holcombe Springs/Shiloh was burned several times during the war and many families fled to Texas to avoid the fighting. In 1868, Holcombe returned and drew up the first plat of the town, and Shiloh Church was rebuilt. In 1872, when the town petitioned for a post office, another Shiloh already existed in the state. Sarah Reed Meek, the wife of James Meek, one of the town fathers, suggested the name

Springdale, short for "springs in the dale." In 1878, the town was incorporated with the name of Springdale.

Transportation was always a challenge for the area, so when the Frisco Railway was built through the town, Springdale really began to boom. Small orchards exploded in size and hundreds of carloads of apples, strawberries, peaches, and grapes were shipped out by rail each year. All of this business caused the center of commerce to move along the railroad tracks and away from the spring. The Western Arkansas Fruit Growers and Shippers Cooperative Association, which organized in Springdale in 1888, provided a surge in growing, producing and marketing activities to the booming orchard industry. By the 1930s, Springdale's industries included the region's only roller mill for producing high-grade flour, bran, and feed; a grape juice plant; a winery and distillery; and canneries. Steele Canning Company, founded by Joe Steele in 1924, grew to be one of the largest privately owned canning companies in the world, partly as a result of the introduction of Popeye brand spinach in 1965. In the early 1930s, John Tyson started the predecessor to Tyson Foods using his old truck to haul chickens out of the area to sell for farmers who owned hatcheries.

Trucking has long been an important industry in the area. Initially, the trucking industry grew primarily out of growers' needs to transport fruit to the canning factories and warehouses, but also to move poultry. For example, Harvey Jones went into the hauling business with a wagon and team of two mules in 1918, which launched Jones Truck Lines. After 1930 when U.S. Highway 71 was paved from Kansas City, Missouri, to Fort Smith, the number of trucking firms increased dramatically. In 2005, there were twenty-six truck lines operating out of Springdale. One of the nation's largest transportation companies in the United States – J.B. Hunt – has its headquarters just north of town.

As the area's population grew, more water was needed. During the early 1960s, Beaver Lake was built to the east of town on the White River. The lake and its recreational facilities attract many tourists each year, making tourism the second-largest economic boon to the area. Today, Springdale is a major industrial center in northwest Arkansas with a population that almost doubled between 1980 and 2000. Springdale has more than seventy-five manufacturing and poultry-processing plants. Springdale is the location of the headquarters of Tyson Foods, the largest meat producing company in the world, and has been dubbed the "Chicken Capital of the World" by several publications.

An interesting feature of Springdale is that it is the home to a Consulate of the Marshall Islands, one of only 11 Marshall Islands diplomatic and consular representations abroad. The Marshall Islands consulate general is one of 1,471 foreign representations in the United States, and the only foreign representation in Springdale. The consulate is located in Springdale since it is the home of between 4,000 and 7,000 Marshallese, making Springdale the site of the largest Marshallese population outside of the Marshall Islands.

For the tourist, there are a number of attractions that should be mentioned. Springdale is the home of the Rodeo of the Ozarks, a Fourth of July rodeo held by the Professional Rodeo Cowboys Association. Started in 1945, this professional rodeo is one of the top twenty-five rodeos in the nation. Parsons Stadium, where the rodeo is held, also features a year-long schedule of family friendly entertainment.

Also located in Springdale is Arvest Ballpark, named in 2008 as the Best New Ballpark in the country. It is the home of the Northwest Arkansas Naturals of the Texas League, having moved here from being the Wichita Wranglers. The Ballpark seats 6,500 and features group and corporate areas in addition to two separate play areas for the kids.

Located on 86 acres on the south edge of Springdale is the Botanical Gardens of the Ozarks. Attracting more than 40,000 visitors a year, the Garden is a collection of ten themed gardens and includes the region's only butterfly house. Located just west of Springdale is Tontitown, the location of several regionally famous Italian restaurants. It is also the home of Tontitown Winery, located in the "Taldo House" built in 1917, and the "Dixie Pride Bonded Winery #40." All of the wines are made on-site from local Tontitown grown grapes. To the east of Springdale is Saddlebock Brewery, the first production brewery in northwest

Arkansas. The brewery produces German-style beers and British and American ales.

For those who want to know more about the area, you can go to downtown Springdale and visit the Shiloh Museum of Ozark History, the "region's premier historical museum that captures the essence of life in the Ozark Mountains and our heritage." The Museum has an outstanding collection of historical photographs as well as other research material.

Arvest Ballpark in Springdale. Photo by Sarah Jennings.

History of the Route of the Arkansas & Missouri Railroad: The St. Louis and San Francisco Railway Company

The St. Louis and San Francisco Railway Co. (StL&SF, or SL-SF), better known as the Frisco, was organized in 1876 in Missouri. The Frisco's first line into Arkansas came south from Monett, Missouri. As was typical at the time, the construction involved a number of "paper" companies coming together to build and initially operate the railroad. The first of these companies was the St. Louis, Arkansas, and Texas Railway Company of Missouri, incorporated June 4, 1880. By summer 1881, the company owned and operated 32 miles of track from Monett to the Missouri-Arkansas state line. The second company involved was incorporated on July 17, 1880. This company, the St. Louis, Arkansas, and Texas Railway Company of Arkansas, built approximately 37 miles of track from the Missouri-Arkansas state line to near Fayetteville.

The line between Monett, Missouri, and Benton County in Arkansas, was under construction during late 1880 and early 1881. The line reached the newly founded town of Rogers, named in honor of the Frisco's general manager, Charles Warrington Rogers, on May 10, 1881. Less than a month later, on June 8, 1881, a passenger train with Charles Rogers aboard entered the northern limits of Fayetteville for the first time.

In September 1880, the Frisco created a third railroad subsidiary, the Missouri, Arkansas and Southern Railway of Arkansas. The new subsidiary was authorized "to build in a southerly direction" – likely from Fayetteville (Washington County) – "to some point on the Little Rock & Fort Smith Railway, not east of Clarksville, with total mileage of about 55 miles." Within a year, the railroad had 63 miles of track under construction between Fayetteville and Fort Smith.

On June 28, 1881, these three railroads were merged to create the St. Louis, Arkansas and Texas Railway Company. By the end of 1881, the Frisco had built south along the West Fork of the White River to its first major obstacle, the mountains near Winslow. A temporary track was built over the hilltop at Winslow while work began on a 1,400-foot-long tunnel, Arkansas' first railroad tunnel. South of the tunnel, the terrain of the route proved just as difficult, with three high trestle bridges built to cross deep hollows in the next 2.5 miles, the tallest of which was 117 feet.

On January 21, 1882, the St. Louis, Arkansas and Texas Railway Company was sold to the St. Louis and San Francisco Railway Company (which became the St. Louis and San Francisco Railroad Company on June 30, 1896). Later, the Fort Smith and Van Buren Bridge Co., capitalized by the Frisco and incorporated in March, 1885, began construction of a bridge over the Arkansas River at Van Buren, finishing it in 1885 and allowing the railway line to continue southwest to Paris, Texas. The bridge was sold to the St. Louis and San Francisco Railroad Company on July 17, 1907.

In 1883, construction continued on south from Fort Smith, through Indian Territory, and on to Paris, Texas (169 miles). The line from Fort Smith to the state line was built by the Ft. Smith and Southern Railway Company. From the state line to Paris, the line was built by the St. Louis and San Francisco Railway Company and the Paris and Great Northern Railroad Company. The Monett to Paris line was completed on July 1, 1887, connecting with the Texas and Pacific to Dallas and Fort Worth.

During the latter part of the nineteenth century, a variety of spurs, branches, and short lines were built off this mainline. The first was a short line run east slightly more than twenty miles from Seligman, Missouri, to the young resort town of Eureka Springs (AR), where the Frisco was instrumental in building the Crescent Hotel. Another spur ran west to Bentonville and eventually continued into the Indian Territory (present-day Oklahoma). Just south of Fayetteville, a short line was built southeast up the White River valley to St. Paul and Pettigrew. This line was designed to get at the hardwoods of the Ozark Mountains to supply the railway company with oak ties as well as feed the booming lumber industry. Another connecting railroad, the Kansas City and Memphis Railroad, ran from Fayetteville to Cave Springs to

History of the Route

the northwest. It became known locally as the "Fruit Belt Line" because of all the apple and peach orchards from which it hauled produce. Another line out of Fayetteville, the Ozark and Cherokee Central, ran west through Farmington, Prairie Grove, and Lincoln to Tahlequah, Oklahoma. For those interested in all of the details, check out the books *Shortline Railroads of Arkansas* by Clifton E. Hull and *Railroads of Northwest Arkansas* by Robert G. Winn. Also, check out *The North Arkansas Line* by James R. Fair, Jr., for information on the Missouri & North Arkansas Railroad.

After the Frisco's improved mainline was built to the west across Oklahoma during the late 1890s and early 1900s, the line between Monett and Fort Smith, and on south to Paris, Texas, took on the role of a secondary line mostly serving local businesses. By 1926, six passenger trains headed west out of Springfield (MO) on a daily basis, but only two turned south at Monett to cover this route, although the Fort Smith route was still part of Table 1 in the *Official Guide*. By 1934, Table 1 was the route through Tulsa, with the Fort Smith route now on Table 1a. In 1949, the Fort Smith route had fallen to Table 5. During this time, there were also two major series of station closures over the route. The first seemed to have happened around 1927, with the second immediately after World War II, centered around 1947. Regular steam service ended on the Monett to Fort Smith line during fall 1950. The last of the steam on this route included a fleet of 2-8-0s. Replacing them were new diesel-powered GP7s and FP7s, which operated well into the 1960s. For many railroad enthusiasts, the line was a throwback route to explore as older equipment and practices tended to hang on longer here. This seemed to continue after the Frisco merged into the Burlington Northern Railroad on November 21, 1980. Because of the line's slow loss of business, the line was determined to be a candidate for a lease-purchase agreement, with it being turned over to the Arkansas & Missouri Railroad in 1986.

As you travel over the railroad, you can see a few foundations and other remnants of the old Frisco. Most notably, look for the Fayetteville, Van Buren, and Fort Smith (AR) passenger depots. The station at Bentonville also still exists. Additionally, a number of old foundations and abandoned right-of-ways can be seen from the train that help recall earlier days.

Frisco Passenger Trains

Passenger service was never heavy on this line, although several trains operated daily over the line during the early years. For example, in the January 1910 *Official Guide*, the line from St. Louis to Fort Smith was Table 1 for the Frisco Lines passenger train listing (odd number trains ran west, even number trains ran east toward St. Louis). While seven trains in each direction were listed as running between St. Louis and Monett, only four were listed between Monett and Fort Smith, with three operating south of Fort Smith. These Monett-Fort Smith trains included #3/#4 – St. Louis to Fort Worth trains, #5/#6 - St. Louis to Dallas trains with through sleepers (electric-lighted) to San Antonio and Galveston, and #11/#12 – long distance locals to Paris (TX) with sleepers set off at Seligman for Eureka Springs. The fourth set of trains were #720/#721 – all stops locals between Fort Smith and Monett, northbound in the morning and southbound in the evening. At the same time, there were three pairs of trains operating between Rogers and Bentonville. Trains #772 and #776 (eastbound) and #775 and #777 (westbound) ran between Grove and Rodgers, while trains #771 and #774 operated only between Rogers and Bentonville. Speed wasn't an issue with these trains as it took 25 minutes or more to make the 5 mile run between Rogers and Bentonville.

In 1926, trains #5/#6 – now known as *The Texas Limited* – still operated over the line with Galveston sleepers. However, trains #3/#4 – *The Ozark Limited* – now ran to Fort Worth via Tulsa, and connecting trains #703/#704 served the route between Monett and Fort Smith. Locals #707/#708 also served the line, southbound midday and northbound in the afternoon, normally meeting at Winslow. There were still six trains daily between Rogers and Bentonville, with new numbers but similar schedules.

History of the Route

By the start of World War II, the mainline saw only one train northbound and southbound each day. The trains, #9-709 and #710-10, connected at Monett with the mainline *Meteor*. Southbound, train #709 generally left Monett before sunrise and arrived in Fort Smith about 8:30am. Northbound, train #710 generally left Fort Smith about 7:00pm and arrived at Monett shortly before midnight. Trains #709 and #710 featured all air-conditioned passenger cars, including a 12 section, 1 drawing room St. Louis-Fort Smith sleeper. Food was provided by a "snack car providing meal service" as the dining car operated on the mainline train only.

In 1946, the trains had been renumbered as #5 and #6 and named the *Twin Meteor*, but their schedules remained similar, with a slightly earlier departure southbound from Monett. The trains featured a St. Louis to Paris sleeping car (12 section-1 drawing room) and a Monett-Paris coach-snack car. However, the St. Louis to Paris sleeper service was discontinued on March 16, 1947.

By 1956, the train was back to being known as the *Meteor* and numbered 9-709 and 704-10. While the southbound train's schedule basically remained unchanged, the northbound train out of Fort Smith now departed at 6:15pm. The sleeper had again been shortened to a St. Louis-Fort Smith run, now using a 10 section-3 double bedroom car. The coach-buffet car also now operated only between Monett and Fort Smith.

In 1958, the last passenger train headed south out of Fort Smith on February 1. This left a simple Monett to Fort Smith passenger turn operating on the most scenic part of the line. These trains operated as trains 9-709 and 910-10 and were still known as the *Meteor*, although locals knew them as the *Meteorite*. The schedules between Monett and Fort Smith remained much the same – an early morning run southbound and an evening run northbound. The train still handled a 10 section-3 double bedroom sleeping car, but no buffet car is mentioned.

By the October 1959 public timetable, the sleeping car had been changed to a 14 roomette-4 double bedroom car, but the schedule had only minor changes. On June 29, 1963, St. Louis to Fort Smith sleeper service ended. Improved roads led to further reductions in the demand for passenger service. The last Frisco passenger train left Fort Smith for Monett on September 18, 1965.

Photo by Sarah Jennings.

Route Guides

Because the Arkansas & Missouri Railroad operates passenger trains over almost its entire system, this book will provide information about all routes that the railroad owns. However, since the A&M primarily operates between Springdale and Van Buren, this territory will be featured initially.

It should be noted that this guide is not designed to be a complete history of the railroad, but instead a great deal of information for those who like to ask "where are we and what once happened here?" Because of this, the guide includes current as well as former station locations, historic towns, and major stream crossing along the line. Stations and industrial tracks currently listed in the Arkansas & Missouri Railroad employee timetable are <u>underlined</u>.

Directions on this railroad will be based upon the railroad's own terminology. A train heading from Springdale to Van Buren is heading south, so to the left is railroad-east, and to the right is railroad-west. Because of the change in direction, and the fact that some passengers may be sitting backwards, the east and west direction will generally be used for the direction to look from the train.

Note that every station and bridge location is also identified by a milepost location. Railroads identify locations along their routes by mileposts, much like highways do. For the Arkansas & Missouri Railroad, the mileposts date back to the Frisco and their distance from St. Louis. There are signs every mile along the railroad that identify this distance. These signs are generally located on the west side of the tracks, so watch for them if you wish.

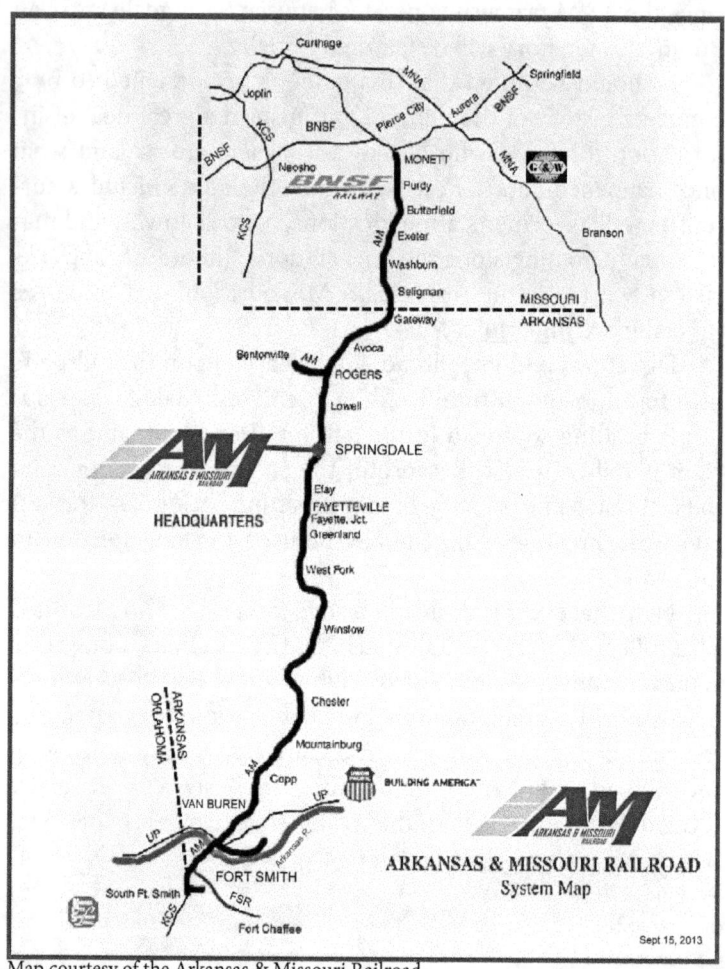

Map courtesy of the Arkansas & Missouri Railroad.

Route Guide: Springdale to Van Buren

The Arkansas & Missouri Railroad operates regular passenger train trips between Springdale and Van Buren, both cities in western Arkansas. This route covers the mountainous terrain between the Ozark Plateau at Springdale and the Arkansas River Valley at Van Buren. Between the two, the railroad climbs over the spine of the Ozark Mountains at Winslow, passing through a tunnel at the highest mountain pass between the Rockies and Appalachians. This route guide includes current as well as former station locations, historic towns, and major stream crossing along the line, listed by milepost. Stations and industrial tracks currently listed in the Arkansas & Missouri Railroad employee timetable are underlined.

343.1   SPRINGDALE – Springdale is the center of operations for the Arkansas & Missouri Railroad. Freight trains operate out of Springdale, both northbound and southbound. These trains include the large trains to Fort Smith (AR) and Monett (MO), as well as numerous locals that serve the railroad between Rogers and Fayetteville.

A&M offices in Springdale. Photo by Sarah Jennings.

On the north side of Emma Street are the various offices of the Arkansas & Missouri Railroad. To their north is the new locomotive shops complex, located east of the tracks. In the same area is a new freight car repair shop, all part of the investments the railroad has brought to the community. This is a working railroad, so please do not trespass into these busy facilities.

Also located north of Emma Street and on the west side of the tracks was once the Frisco station. Built in 1923 of brick, it was 196 feet long and 37 feet wide. It featured the waiting rooms and office on its south end with a very large freight room on the north end. The Frisco gave Springdale the telegraph code "SA". Torn down in 1982, the station was replaced by a metal building (still used by the A&M) built by Burlington Northern the same year. All of the remaining BN agents in northwest Arkansas (Bentonville, Rogers and Springdale) were centralized in this building.

A&M Passenger Depot in Springdale. Photo by Sarah Jennings.

Passengers board their passenger train at a new passenger station south of Emma Street near downtown Springdale. Passenger ticketing, restrooms, and a gift shop are all located in this station. Adjacent is the

Route Guide: Springdale to Van Buren

new railroad museum full of historic displays, generally open for viewing before and after all passenger trains.

For the history of Springdale, check out the Introduction to Springdale section of this trip guide.

343.4 SPRING CREEK – The railroad crosses this small stream on an 83-foot long I-beam bridge. The origins of Springdale started on the banks of Spring Creek.

Alongside Spring Creek is the Northwest Arkansas Razorback Greenway, a "36-mile, primarily off-road, shared-use trail that extends from the Bella Vista Trail in north Bentonville to south Fayetteville." Funding for the trail primarily came from the Walton Family Foundation and a federal transportation grant. This is the first of several crossings of this trail by the railroad.

345.3 U.S. HIGHWAY 71 – The railroad crosses the old main highway on this through plate girder bridge. The railroad has started on a downhill grade heading south, generally exceeding 1% (one foot change in elevation for one hundred feet of track) all the way to Clear Creek at Johnson. North of here, the railroad passed by the large George's poultry facility. Based in Springdale, George's is a fourth generation, privately held organization that is still led by the George family. The company is among the largest poultry producers in the world and is a regular customer of the railroad

To the south of the overpass is another large shipper on the railroad. Here, the headquarters of Tyson Foods can be seen to the west of the railroad. Founded in 1935, Tyson Foods is one of the world's largest processors and marketers of beef, chicken, and pork (sales are in that order), as well as prepared foods such as appetizers and snacks. In 2010, they were the largest producer of both beef and chicken, and the second largest producer of pork, in the United States. They sell their products to customers in more than 100 countries.

346.6 SHADY GROVE ROAD – The Tyson feed mill to the west may be the most photographed structure on the railroad. The view across the open pasture on the left has been a "must do" photograph ever since the A&M started.

Track Warrant Control (TWC) starts just north of here at milepost 346.4, and covers the territory south to milepost 407.5 near Copp. TWC is a verbal authorization system used to authorize trains to occupy Main Tracks. The system permits a specific train to occupy a specific piece of main track between named locations.

347.4 JOHNSONS – While the town is Johnson, the railroad has known this location as Johnsons, or Johnson Station. While Johnson wasn't incorporated until 1961, the first record of business activity here was 1830-1834 when John Trusdale purchased a mill site west of present-day Johnson from a "widow Sutton." In 1835, he built a gristmill utilizing the water flow from a number of springs north of the property. The mill was burned during the Civil War in 1864. Following the Civil War, Jacob Queener Johnson and William Mays purchased the site and rebuilt the mill in 1865. In about 1884, Mayes sold his share of the mill to B. F. Johnson, brother of J. Q. Johnson. The Johnson Mill operated until 1985 when, due to declining health, Frank Johnson (grandson of B. F. Johnson) closed the mill. Today, the renovated facility is the Inn at the Mill, a hotel.

The Frisco opened for service in Johnson (telegraph code JO) on June 8, 1881, in part due to pressure from strawberry growers in the area who formed the Johnson Fruitmen's Union to ship out fruit and berries in bulk on the railroad. In 1900, Washington County reported 2,429 acres of strawberries under cultivation with many in the Johnson area. The Union also shipped carloads of grapes grown in the area. The Fruitmen's Union lasted until trucks took the business.

Route Guide: Springdale to Van Buren

The village of Johnson secured a post office in 1886 which seemed to bounce around from home to home and business to business for quite some time. The old post office can be seen to the east of the tracks. Look for the old white building that once was also a general store.

A frame depot was also in this area, built in 1902 and similar to other area Frisco stations, such as the one at Avoca. The Johnson station was located on the west side of the tracks. Today there is a short siding to the east of the mainline that is often used by the yearly Springdale to Johnson Santa Claus trains, was well as numerous fright trains.

347.7   **GULLEY** – From 1903 to 1939, there was a 19-car spur into lime works nearby. Some records show the company to be the Fayetteville White Lime Works.

348.0   **CLEAR CREEK BRIDGE** – This bridge is 202 feet long. It consists of a deck plate girder with ballast deck pile trestles on each end, typical for this rail line. Clear Creek is at 1,172 feet of elevation and at the bottom of grades in both directions, about 1% to the north to Springdale and between 0.6% and 1.15% south to Fayetteville. Clear Creek starts to the east. It provides water to Lake Fayetteville before flowing west through Johnson, and then further west into the Illinois River.

348.2   **ZERO MOUNTAIN** – The Crescent White Lime Company purchased land along Clear Creek in 1897. In 1903, the name was changed to the Ozark White Lime Company. At one time, the company operated two lime plants, which used a total of five kilns to burn the rock for processing into lime. Each kiln burned enough rock to produce approximately 400 barrels of lime daily. Photos of the limestone caves show tracks with small mining carts being used.

The caves of the former limestone quarries were converted into underground cold storage facilities by

Zero Mountain, which, in 1955, began receiving frozen products for storage. Founded in Johnson, the company is now based in Fort Smith and has storage units in four northwest Arkansas locations, including the original site here.

349.3 U.S. HIGHWAY 71 – The railroad passes under this highway which connects Interstate 49 with the U.S. 71 Business Route through the downtowns of Springdale and Fayetteville.

350.1 BARBARA – Look for the Jocelyn Lane road crossing. Some records show that this location was originally called Lilburn. Apparently, there was an 11-car spur west of the mainline from about 1905 to 1950. To the east is the Whistle Stop Plaza, with a caboose included in the facility. The caboose was built as Erie C103, and was later sold to the Wellsville, Addison and Galeton Railroad as their C103. The caboose then went to the Louisiana & North West Railroad as 213, before becoming Arkansas & Missouri 170.

Just north of here, the Razorback Greenway and the Scull Creek Trail follow Scull Creek under the Arkansas & Missouri Railroad tracks. Scull Creek Trail is considered as the base of the Fayetteville trails and is the core of the Razorback Greenway. Scull Creek is sometimes known as Skull Creek.

351.9 EFAY – Known as East Fayetteville, there has long been a short spur here to the west, and once a siding to the east. Just south of the location of the former south switch is another bridge over Scull Creek, and the Scull Creek Trail.

352.3 FAYETTEVILLE STATION SWITCH – A switch to the east once led to a spur for the Fayetteville Frisco station. At one time, the track went across Dickson Street and headed on south a mile or so and then turned to the

Route Guide: Springdale to Van Buren

west and passed under the Frisco mainline, and continued on west (today, much of this route is now a walking path known as the Frisco Trail). When the A&M took over the railroad, only the line south of former U.S. Highway 62 (now Arkansas Highway 180/45) still existed, used to serve a small feed mill, reached from the McNair switch at 353.8. Today, even this has been abandoned and the mill area has been replaced by a large apartment complex.

The Fayetteville station switch is located at the top of a grade from both directions. Heading on south, the mainline grade drops at 1% all the way to Fayette Junction.

352.4 **FAYETTEVILLE** – When the railroad arrived in 1882, it built the first depot, which was of frame construction. It burned down in 1896 and a brick station was built to replace it. The station still standing in Fayetteville is one of the few original Frisco stations left on the Arkansas & Missouri. Located on West Dickson, the Frisco station (telegraph code FA) was built in 1897, then rebuilt in 1926 after the second station again suffered damage from a fire. Made of stucco and brick, it is listed on the National Register of Historic Places (listed August 12, 1988). The original brick station was one building, but the new station includes a separate freight room and boiler room building to the north of the station. The station also once included a Frisco Line Harvey Newsstand.

The December 8, 1926, issue of the *Fayetteville Daily Democrat* stated:

> "Plans are being made by local Frisco officials to occupy the new station shortly after the Christmas holidays, according to an announcement made Wednesday morning. The building has been in the course of construction on West Dickson for the past three months.

The new station is of the Spanish type with the exterior of red face brick and white stucco. The roof is built of red tile with terra cotta trimmings and a stone plate at each end of the station bears the word 'Fayetteville.' An expenditure of between $40,000 and $45,000 is represented, contractors said Wednesday.

Workmen are busy completing a large platform which will measure more than 600 feet north of Dickson Street and about 135 feet south. The south platform will be used in exchanging baggage and express on southbound trains.

The floor of the new structure will be of concrete and the rooms beautifully decorated it is said. All the furniture will be new, including tables and instruments that will be used in the ticket agent's office. A portico has been built at the south end of the building and a large spacious baggage and express room has been built on the north.

Building work is in charge of W. C. Staver of Kansas City, railroad construction concern."

When built, there were two stub tracks between the main line and the freight house. The track next to the freight house handled the freight business, while the western of the two stub tracks was used by the passenger trains of the Ozark & Cherokee Central Railway, later the Frisco Muskogee Branch.

Rail service helped build the Fayetteville area, and the Frisco was the dominant force in the region. While a number of independent railroads were proposed for the area, and some even built, the Frisco eventually controlled most of them. The Pacific & Great Eastern Railroad Company was incorporated on October 23, 1884, and proposed to build across the state but only built a line from Fayetteville to Wyman, twelve miles east of here. However, the line didn't last long. The Frisco soon controlled a branch line to St. Paul and Pettigrew in Madison County. The St. Paul branch provided a great amount of hardwood for processing into railroad ties, furniture, handles, and various other wood products. About 1900, construction started from Fayetteville to the west on the Ozark & Cherokee Central Railway. It was first completed to Westville, Oklahoma, and later extended to Tahlequah and Muskogee, Oklahoma. The line was later purchased by the SLSF.

While looking at the former Frisco station, look for the bank to the east which was built using railroad cars. The passenger car was once owned by the New York Central Railroad and was acquired from the former Little Rock Chapter of the National Railway Historical Society. The wooden caboose is ex-Cotton Belt, reportedly also once owned by the Warren & Saline River Railroad. The caboose is the office of the loan department.

The first settlers arrived at today's Fayetteville during the mid-1820s and settled at several springs near Mount Sequoyah. By the late 1820s, the Leeper family owned much of the area with Matthew Leeper being appointed the receiver of the Land Office by President Andrew Jackson. When Washington County was created in 1828, this area became the county seat and was known as Washington Courthouse. On June 16, 1834, President Andrew Jackson authorized the patent for the land, soon to be Fayetteville. In 1835, the President issued the patent that established the original town on February 27. The first use of the name Fayetteville reportedly came about in 1829 when a post office was established. Two commissioners locating the county seat came from Fayetteville, Tennessee, and urged the postmaster to name it after that community.

Fayetteville was soon a center of regional education. The Fayetteville Female Academy was incorporated on October 26, 1836, and was the second school chartered by the state. The Arkansas College of Fayetteville opened in 1850 and was chartered on December 14, 1852. The first bachelor's degrees in the state were granted by the college, and the college was soon given the power to confer doctoral degrees. Finally, on December 16, 1858, the state chartered the Fayetteville Female Institute.

The Dickson Street area began to boom with the coming of the railroad, becoming a commercial, lodging, shipping, and packing center. Today, this entire area is part of the West Dickson Street Commercial Historic District, known locally as simply Dickson Street. This area is one of the oldest parts of Fayetteville, and has seen everything from Civil War battles to busy commerce to the depths of depression. Today, it is home to the Walton Arts Center, unique shops, multiple bars and restaurants, new condo projects, and the *Bikes, Blues, and BBQ* bike festival – the third largest motorcycle rally in the country. Dickson Street is generally considered to be one of the two most popular entertainment districts in the state, along with the River Market district in downtown Little Rock.

As the Arkansas Historic Preservation Program states, "The history of Dickson Street dates back to the original survey of the town in 1835, with present-day Dickson Street serving as the northern boundary. Dickson Street was named for one of the early families in Fayetteville, the Joseph L. Dickson (1817-1868) family." Dickson moved to this area when his father received a promotion to United States Land Registrar by President James K. Polk. Joseph L. Dickson was a merchant and financier in Fayetteville during the 1840s and 50s. Dickson owned a large mercantile, flour mill, and home on what became Dickson Street. During the Civil War, his home (located where the Central United Methodist Church now stands) served as a hospital.

On April 16, 1863, the Confederate army attacked Union forces at Fayetteville in what became known as the Battle of Fayetteville. Troops fought at what is present-day College and Dickson Streets to the east in a

Route Guide: Springdale to Van Buren

battle that left few men dead but left the place with the name "Bloody Corner."

The Morrill Act, passed by Congress during the war, provided land grants to each state to establish agricultural and mechanical colleges. Upon reentering the Union, Arkansas became eligible for the grants. Washington County proposed a $100,000 bond issue and Fayetteville offered another $30,000, including individual land donations, to build a college. Fayetteville's proposal was selected, and Arkansas Industrial University opened on January 22, 1872. In 1899, the legislature changed the name to the University of Arkansas.

In 1924, the University of Arkansas erected a wireless apparatus and began broadcasting as KFMQ radio, later changed to KUOA. It is recognized as one of the oldest radio stations in the world. The University sold KUOA to a commercial company in 1933 who in turn sold it to John Brown University in nearby Siloam Springs, Arkansas.

353.3 **WEST SIXTH STREET** – This street has a lot of names, including West 6th Street and Martin Luther King Jr. Boulevard. It is also Arkansas Highways 45 and 180. Before 1995, the railroad used a 135-foot steel stringer bridge to cross the road, but it was replaced by a new bridge in that year.

353.4 **O&CC UNDERPASS** – The Ozark & Cherokee Central track once passed under the Frisco mainline here. When the A&M acquired the line, part of the line still went under the tracks here to serve a small mill and farm supply store a few blocks to the east. Today, the area to the east has been redeveloped into an apartment complex and the line is gone. However, the railroad grade under the A&M is now the Tsa-La-Gi Trail. Tsa-La-Gi reportedly means "Cherokee" in the Cherokee language, and the trail supporters envision it heading west to Oklahoma.

353.8 McNAIR – This was the junction with the Muskogee Subdivision, the line that once went west to Westville (AR) and Muskogee (OK), built as the Ozark & Cherokee Central. A short bit of track still exists here to serve a cement plant. The name McNair honors W. P. McNair, the Fayetteville station agent from 1886 until 1917.

The Ozark & Cherokee Central began in 1900 as the North Arkansas & Western Railway when a few businessmen in the Fayetteville area proposed to build a railroad from Fayetteville westward to the Illinois River Valley in Indian Territory (Oklahoma). While the railroad had a goal of reaching Tahlequah after crossing the KCS at Westville, a lack of funding required its reorganization as the O&CC. It took several contractors using convict labor to build the line between Fayetteville and the Indian Territory, but the railroad was soon extended on to Muskogee and Okmulgee, connecting with the Frisco also on its west end.

A *New York Times* article in the April 15, 1903, edition stated that the O&CC had acquired the Shawnee, Oklahoma & Missouri Coal and Railway Company and had just received permission from the Arkansas Railroad Commission to extend the line 400 miles by building eastward from Fayetteville to Jasper (Arkansas), westward into Oklahoma City, and a new line from Muskogee into Fort Smith. With the railroad's almost immediate success, the Frisco acquired it in 1903. In 1926, the railroad was operating two sets of passenger trains between Fayetteville and Muskogee – a morning and an afternoon train in each direction. However, the line didn't boom much further and much of the line, known as the Muskogee Subdivision, was abandoned in 1942 under the order of the War Production Authority.

To the east is the former Campbell Soup plant. In March 1998, the facility became one of the largest plants operated by Vlasic Foods International when Campbell Soup Company spun off the Vlasic Foods division. Vlasic controlled the Swanson TV dinners, Open Pit and

Route Guide: Springdale to Van Buren

Vlasic Pickles brands. In 2003, it acquired Aurora Foods and soon became Pinnacle Foods. In 2009, Pinnacle Foods acquired Birds Eye Foods, Inc. Today, the company, which went public in 2013, controls brands such as Duncan Hines, Vlasic, Birds Eye, Van de Kamp's, Mrs Paul's, Aunt Jemima, and Armour and Company. The basic goal of the company is to reinvigorate iconic brands.

354.4 **TOWN BRANCH BRIDGE** – This 154-foot long bridge crosses the Town Branch, which flows east into the Cato Springs Branch.

354.5 **FAYETTE JUNCTION** – During Frisco days, this was telegraph station FJ. This is the former junction with the line to the east to the Arkansas communities of Pettigrew, Combs, and Cass. The line was originally chartered on September 4, 1886, as the Fayetteville & Little Rock Railroad by Hugh F. McDanield, who built it to log the mountains to the east to supply railroad ties to the Frisco.

The switch at this location was first installed on December 4, 1886, and the location was immediately named Fayette Junction. By February, 1887, the line had been built to Powell, about twenty-five miles east. On February 23, 1887, the Frisco acquired the railroad. By the end of the year, dozens of sawmills were cutting wood along the line. In 1897, the line was extended further east to Pettigrew ("Hardwood Capital of the World") to reach new timber stands. More than a dozen lumber and stave mills operated in Pettigrew within a year. The Arkansas timber industry peaked in 1909 when more than two billion board feet of lumber was cut in the state.

As the timber was cut, farming took over. Soon the railroad was hauling local products such as apples, various vegetables, and livestock. However, there was still plenty of timber in the area, and in January 1915, the

Black Mountain & Eastern Railroad was incorporated to build from Combs, on the St. Paul Branch, southward to Cass (20 miles) to serve the needs of the J. H. Phipps Lumber Company. In reality, the railroad had already been built starting in 1912, but without the authorization of the Arkansas Railroad Commission. The largest timber company in the region, Phipps Lumber had sawmills and production plants in Combs, Pettigrew, and Fayetteville. Much of the timber hauled on the Black Mountain & Eastern was used to manufacture ties and bridge materials.

In 1916, the name of the BM&E was changed to the Combs, Cass & Eastern. William Fulbright, later the Arkansas senator who sponsored the Fulbright Scholar Program, became a director of the Combs, Cass & Eastern in 1923 at the legal minimum age of 18. The Fulbright family had obtained control of the J. H. Phipps Lumber Company and its railroad in 1920. However, the CC&E was abandoned during the mid-1920s after the timber was all removed. The Phipps Company later became part of Fulbright Industries and continued to manufacture wood products, including wagons and furniture, for decades.

In 1926, the Frisco ran a daily train (#769) departing Fayetteville at 8:15am to Pettigrew, arriving at noon. The train came back as #768, departing Pettigrew at 1:00pm and arriving at Fayetteville at 4:15pm. The St. Paul Branch, as the Frisco called the railroad, was abandoned in late July 1937. Although abandoned more than 75 years ago, the grade is still visible in many places along its route.

There was once a yard and engine terminal at Fayette Junction to serve the branch and other area lines, however it was closed in 1950 as local service in the area was reduced. There is a short siding to the west, and a wye track still exists to the east. When the A&M was first created, the line went 2.7 miles to the east, serving a scrapyard (Ozark Steel) and a small industry (Sim-

Route Guide: Springdale to Van Buren

mons). There were two small timber bridges, both in poor shape. Eventually, this line was abandoned by the railroad during the early 1990s.

354.8 **CATO SPRINGS BRANCH BRIDGE** – Cato Springs Branch is a beautiful, northeast-flowing tributary of the Town Branch. On a number of maps, this stream is also shown as Town Branch further downstream. There was once a small community located about 2 miles southwest of Fayetteville known as Cato Springs.

355.2 **U.S. HIGHWAY 71** – The railroad passes under this highway which connects Interstate 49 with the U.S. 71 Business Route through the downtowns of Springdale and Fayetteville. South of here, U.S. 71 follows the railroad to the east across the mountains and all the way to Van Buren. Once the main highway in the area, today it is known as the Boston Mountains Scenic Loop and is a beautiful drive.

357.8 **GREENLAND** – Look for Wilson Street as this was where the depot once stood on the east side of the tracks. The original frame depot was built in 1906 as a 40'x24' four-room building with a cinder platform. A long siding once existed on the west side of the mainline, stretching between the bridges on the north and south side of town. Trains heading south start facing a grade which stiffens to more than 1% as they approach Winslow Tunnel. The railroad follows the West Fork of the White River all the way to Winslow. You are technically entering the Boston Mountains, part of the Ozarks.

The Boston Mountains are the southwestern part of the Ozark Plateau, located in western Arkansas and eastern Oklahoma. For the geologist, this area includes the highest, most rugged, and least denuded portion of the Ozarks. This condition is due to their relatively young age. Looking at the deep valleys, the tops of the highest hills are from the flat-lying sedimentary layers of the Paleozoic age (251 million to 542 million years ago). This rock is known as Pennsylvanian sandstone and shale. Below them can be seen Mississippian limestones and below that layer Ordovician dolomites.

Mountain tops in the Boston Mountains reach just over 2,560 feet with valleys 500 to 1,550 feet deep. A number of rivers start in this area, including the White River, the Buffalo River, the Kings River, the Illinois River, the Mulberry River, Lee Creek, Frog Bayou, Big Piney Creek, Illinois Bayou, the Little Red River, War Eagle Creek, and Little Mulberry Creek.

In 1828, the federal government reached an agreement with the Cherokee in which the Indians were removed from Lovely County (including later counties of Benton and Washington), Arkansas. The government then urged white settlers to homestead here. The White River valley near what is now Greenland became a popular area for homesteaders. Greenland was first called Frog Pond, the name was changed to Rugby (1882-1886) by the Frisco. Then, Greenland's name was changed to Staunton (1886-1909). In 1909 the town became Greenland.

Fruit production was a primary income for the farms and hillsides around Greenland. Many small landowners grew strawberries – thousands of pounds of strawberries were loaded and shipped from Greenland's railroad depot. Other cash crops included raspberries, blackberries, and apples.

Greenland is the home of the Fayetteville Municipal Airport, also known as Drake Field, mostly replaced by the new Northwest Arkansas Regional Airport which opened on November 1, 1998. Fayetteville's first airport opened in 1927, but a better facility was desired. Dr. Noah Fields Drake was named chairman of the airport committee which bought more land and started a modernization program just before World War II. On April 14, 1947, the airport was named for Dr. Drake. Fayetteville Municipal Airport was an aviator training post

Route Guide: Springdale to Van Buren

during World War II. Located here is the Arkansas Air & Military Museum with its display of world-famous racing planes of the 1920s and 1930s, early commercial aircraft, Vietnam-era Army helicopters, a Navy carrier fighter, and many displays of original artifacts and aviation memorabilia. The museum is famous as one of the few remaining all-wood, 1940s-era aircraft hangars.

362.0   **ROBINSON'S BRANCH BRIDGE** – This bridge is a through plate girder with ballast deck pile trestles on each end, for a total of 162 feet. Robinson's Branch is a short stream starting on the hillside to the southwest.

362.9   <u>WEST FORK</u> – There is a short spur to the east generally used by area track gangs and equipment. The name West Fork was applied to at least two early settlements along the spring-fed headwaters of the West Fork of the White River. Settlers arrived by 1828, creating self-sufficient homesteads farmed by extended family groups. The present location is distinguished by a high bluff along the east side of the river, with the town site in a fertile valley west of the stream. It became the center of village life around 1876 with the construction of a water mill and steam mill across from the bluff. The first West Fork post office was established in 1848, four miles south at a small settlement alternatively named Woolsey and Pitkin, and was relocated to the "new" West Fork in 1878. Thomas McKnight was said to have laid out the town in 1883, which was incorporated in May of 1885, with J. M. Phillips as mayor.

    If you wanted to send a telegram or message to West Fork, the telegraph code was a logical "WF". The station, built in 1884, was located to the east of the mainline and was a two-story wooden structure (60'x24') with living quarters on the second floor.

    Since the completion of Interstate 49, West Fork has seen a small boom as the west side of town is now easily reached and serves as a home for many Fayetteville-area workers.

365.8 WOOLSEY – Look for the grade crossing with Woolsey Road. Some early sources show the station as Woolseys (1881-1905). The Woolsey family settled in this area during the late 1830s-early 1840s. While once an area known for fruit and timber production, today this area is used for hay production, cattle, and chicken farming. There was a post office at Woolsey from 1928 to 1955. Station plans show that this was another typical 32'x20' frame four-room depot (built 1911), except a small fifth room was crammed into the structure to serve as the post office, using part of the "Negro Waiting Room" space. The depot was located on the east side of the tracks.

To the east is the Woolsey Bridge, listed on the National Register of Historic Places. The 303-foot long bridge, built in 1925, carries Washington County Road 35, also known as Woolsey Road, over the West Fork of the White River. The bridge is a rare two-span camelback-through truss, a modification of the Pratt truss designed by Charles H. Parker which features a top chord that is not parallel to the bottom chord. Although stronger in the center than parallel bridges, the style is less common due to its complexity.

Just west of Woolsey is Pitkin Corner, named for the Pitkin family who lived in this area. A post office once existed here, but later moved to West Fork. Pitkin is the name for a layer of limestone throughout the Ozarks. The limestone was first explored and named for exposures near the Pitkin post office in Washington County, Arkansas. Pitkin Chert is also named for the Pitkin area. This stone is usually a solid jet black but can be a dark brown and have lighter inclusions. Reportedly, Native Americans loved this material to make long points or knives.

366.2 WINN CREEK BRIDGE – This bridge is 273 feet long with ballast deck pile trestle spans on each end of a single deck plate girder span. Winn Creek forms about 15 miles to the south and flows northward before entering the West Fork of the White River just a few hundred feet to the east. Winn Creek was named after Minor H. Winn, who along with his wife Matilda, settled here in 1836 and died sometime after 1840 on their farm.

367.0 CLARY – Clary was a short siding named for L. B. Clary, an Assistant General Manager on the Frisco during the 1940s. Some records show that the track was built here in 1944. Look for the wide grade to the east near several small private crossings. The West Fork of the White River is immediately to the east, and will be to near Winslow.

370.0 BRENTWOOD – The Brentwood post office existed here 1881-1964 (the same years that documents show this as a Frisco station), then it became the Brentwood Rural Station (1964-1968). The post office was located in the depot for many years. The depot was built in 1900 as a two-story frame 60'x24' building with living space above the office and waiting rooms. It was located on the east side of the tracks. For a while, the location was known as Gunter.

Brentwood is known for its winter bluegrass shows. The Brentwood Community Center sponsors these shows the 1st and 3rd Saturday nights of the month from October through April. While the public show is popular with the audience, the real action is in the back room where musicians from across the country come to simply jam.

374.0 TRACK SIDE WARNING DETECTOR – This detector is placed to inspect a southbound train before it enters the Winslow Tunnel. If a defect is identified, the detector puts out a solid tone on the railroad's radio. No defects are indicated by a series of short tones. Technology such as this is common in the railroad industry and is designed to make sure brakes and wheel bearings don't overheat and that crews are notified should a wheel of a car derail. For those that wish to listen in, tune your radio scanner to 160.440, channel 22 as assigned by the Association of American Railroads (AAR).

374.7 **WINSLOW** - Elijah J. Woolum established the Woolum-Brown Stage Line operating between Fayetteville and Alma sometime after the Civil War. The stage stop near present day Winslow became known as Summit Home. On December 11, 1876, an application was granted for a post office at Summit Home. A second application to the U.S. Post Office Department on August 3, 1881, changed the town's post office name to Winslow, named for Edward F. Winslow, then-president of the St. Louis-San Francisco Railroad.

Soon after, Fort Smith physician Albert Dunlap visited the area, and in 1887, he built a home here and moved his family to Winslow. Dunlap encouraged others to summer in the cooler mountain area of Winslow. During the early 1900s, Thomas B. Harris developed the Winslow Park Club on a mountain east of town. It had a main lodge and thirty-nine individual cottages owned by families who spent summers in Winslow. On October 3, 1904, the citizens filed a petition to incorporate the city of Winslow, and a charter was granted on February 17, 1905. Today, Winslow is considered to be the highest incorporated town in Arkansas at 1,729 feet above sea level.

The station was located on the east side of the tracks, just south of the main crossing. Part of the passenger platform is still visible north of the crossing. A wooden boardwalk once ran from the depot all the way to the tunnel's north portal. The depot (built 1898) was a twin of the Brentwood depot, except that the freight room was on the north end of the station and there was an

Route Guide: Springdale to Van Buren

additional 36'x20' covered platform next to the waiting room on the south end of the station.

The Winslow Tunnel was protected by Automatic Block Signaling, or ABS, a requirement of state law. ABS is a type of railroad signaling system that consists of a series of signals that divide a railway line into a series of sections, or blocks. The system controls the movement of trains through each block. ABS has the ability to determine if the block ahead is occupied by another train or an obstruction such as a broken rail or rock slide. The ABS located here was to provide more safety for trains passing through Winslow Tunnel and operating on the steep grades to the south. ABS was in effect from milepost 374-35 to 380-34. This is between the sidings of Winslow and Schaberg. The Winslow siding, located to the west, has generally been reported as being 2,142 feet long. The station at Winslow had the telegraph code of "WS".

374.9 **NORTH PORTAL WINSLOW TUNNEL** – Winslow Tunnel was built between 1881 and 1882 and enlarged in 1968 by Morrison Knudsen, increasing the height to twenty-four feet and the width to nineteen feet to permit the use of larger freight cars. A principal challenge of the 1968 work was replacing a massive brick lining that the Frisco installed in the Winslow Tunnel in 1898 and 1899. The original tunnel was finished in July 1882 and train service began operating through it in August. Located at an elevation of 1,735 feet, it is the highest railroad pass between the Rockies and Appalachians. Its length varies by source but they vary between 1,693 and 1,702 feet before the tunnel portals were installed.

Work started on the tunnel on September 26, 1881, with the holing through on June 24, 1882. The tunnel was completed on July 27, 1882. During its construction, the railroad operated a switchback over the top of the hill to get supplies further down the line. The 1882 Frisco Annual Report stated the "Winslow tunnel was the most expensive and difficult part of the work" in building the Arkansas Division to Van Buren. Construction on the tunnel worked from both ends. The *Rogers New Era* newspaper kept a reporter at the head of construction of the railroad and reported often on the construction of the tunnel. In one article, the paper reported that, "Some 75 Irishmen and 400 Kansas negroes are working on the Frisco tunnel through the mountain south of Fayetteville." Other reports stated that due to violence that often erupted between different ethnic groups, all of the line camps were segregated. At the Winslow tunnel, the white workers were based in the community of Winslow while the black workers lived in rough camps on the south side of the mountain.

South Portal Winslow Tunnel. Photo by Barton Jennings.

375.3 SOUTH PORTAL WINSLOW TUNNEL – Once a train exits the south portal, heading southbound, the engineer had better have things under control as the grade varies from 2.1% to 2.3% downhill all the way to Schaberg. From there, the line drops at about 1% all the way to Mountainburg. With many loaded freights heading north, this hill is a long hard climb.

Route Guide: Springdale to Van Buren

The grades of a railroad are very important. According to an article in the September 2011 issue of *Trains Magazine*, "a 2.2 percent climb was considered the standard maximum grade for a well-engineered mountain railroad." Even at this level, trains often required additional locomotives to get up the hill. Helper locomotives, designed to provide extra power to push or pull trains up the hill, often operated between Schaberg and Winslow, adding to the number of train movements in this area.

From here south to near Rudy, the Ozark National Forest includes lands to the east and west of the railroad. The Ozark National Forest covers 1.2 million acres, mostly in the Ozark mountains of northern Arkansas.

Trestle #1. Photo by Barton Jennings.

376.5 **TRESTLE #1** – Trestle #1 stands 125 feet high and is 780 feet long. The BN knew the trestle as Boston Mountain Viaduct #1. It is made up of a series of 13 deck plate girder spans, installed in 1909. There are reports that these three trestles were originally timber but other sources say they were steel and wrought iron when built in 1882. Construction photos show timber trestles being used to build the first bridge, likely causing the various reports.

The railroad here is at 1,566 feet above sea level and is dropping fast as it heads south. Down below is a small wet-weather stream with no name.

377.3 TRESTLE #2 – This bridge is also known as Boston Mountain Viaduct #2 and is 421 feet long and 110 feet tall. It consists of seven deck plate girder spans, installed in 1909. Trestle #2 crosses a dry wash that during rains moves water to Clear Creek to the east,

To the east is Gaylor Mountain, elevation of 2,012 feet. The nearby community that is sometimes visible when the leaves are off the trees is known as Mt. Gayler. This community was very busy with various tourist attractions before Interstate 49 was built. Notice the spelling difference between the mountain and the community. Local legend says that the family the mountain is named for split during a family feud, with those staying on the mountain spelling their name Gaylor while those who left and settled in the town spelled it Gayler.

Trestle #3. Photo by Barton Jennings.

378.2 TRESTLE #3 – This bridge is 110 feet tall and 451 feet long. Rebuilt using seven deck plate girder spans in 1900, it was known as Boston Mountain Viaduct #3.

Route Guide: Springdale to Van Buren

Just north of Trestle #3 is a new slide area, one that took weeks for the A&M to stabilize. This bridge is at an elevation of 1,396 feet above sea level. Below is another wet-weather creek that flows east into Clear Creek.

378.5 **WASHINGTON COUNTY/CRAWFORD COUNTY LINE** – To the north is **Washington County**, created in 1828 and named after George Washington. The county was created from lands known as "Lovely's Purchase," comprised of Osage Indian lands and purchased in 1816 and given to the Cherokee Indians for settlement a year later. By the late 1820s, white settlers were allowed to settle in Lovely's Purchase. Fayetteville is the county seat and home of the University of Arkansas.

Located south of here, **Crawford County** was formed in western Arkansas in 1820 from parts of Pulaski County, which once extended well into what is now Oklahoma. When Crawford County was created, it contained a large part of what is now the State of Oklahoma. The county was named after William Crawford, U.S. Secretary of War in 1815. The county seat is Van Buren.

378.7 **GRAVE SITE** – To the east is the site of a mass grave, reportedly for railroad construction workers who died from smallpox. In early 1882, an outbreak of smallpox swept through the tunnel workforce of 300 men and caused dozens of deaths. Untreated smallpox has a mortality rate of up to thirty percent. After a spring of smallpox, the warmer weather of summer brought with it malaria. Black laborers, working on the south end of the tunnel, were buried in four area graveyards along the railroad, one called the "African Center." Meanwhile, whites worked on the north end of the tunnel and were buried in a whites-only graveyard.

380.8 **TRACK SIDE WARNING DETECTOR** – This detector is placed to inspect a northbound train before it enters the Winslow Tunnel. If a defect is identified, the detector puts out a solid tone on the railroad radio. No defects are indicated by a series of short tones.

In this area the railroad passes through several large cuts created when the railroad built along the side of this mountain. The largest is known as Schaberg Cut and is located less than a mile north of Schaberg.

381.0   SCHABERG – Look for the old WPA-built schoolhouse turned private home to the west. The June 1893 *Travelers' Official Guide* listed this location as Porter, maps also show it as Frisco. Copies of the Frisco Consolidated Station List states that the station of Porter existed from 1884 until 1910. The Schaberg family lived here during the late 1800s and early 1900s and it is reported that at least one member of the family served as station agent. The elevation here is approximately 1,080 feet above sea level.

A&M 44S at Schaberg. Photo by Barton Jennings.

The Washington County Historical Society has published some information on Schaberg. Their information came from the book *History of Crawford Coun-*

ty, by Eula Hopkins and Wanda Gray. The book states that the community was originally known as Porter Village. Soon after the railroad was completed, Porter had three stores, a hotel, and a railway station with operator whose agent lived in the second floor of the depot. The depot was built in 1882 and was the typical 60'x24' station.

Even though the community was originally known as Porter, when a post office was established in April of 1883, it was called Frisco. Mr. Benjamin Strong was appointed the first Postmaster at that time, followed by John W. Schaberg in January of 1888. At this time the community had a population of about a hundred and fifty people. In 1912, the name of the post office was changed to Schaberg. In 1950, postal service was discontinued.

There are reports that there was originally a turntable located at Schaberg for turning helper engines, with a sister turntable at Winslow. In the late 1890s, a fire damaged the turntable and it was moved to Chester as helpers were now based there. Reportedly the turntable at Winslow was abandoned in the early 1900s. This then required helpers to back down the mountain after a shove up the grade.

Through the 1960s at least, a long siding existed at Schaberg for train meets. During this time, Frisco employee timetables included the instructions: *"TRAIN MEET SIGN" opposite south end of siding Schaberg. Northward train holding main track to meet southward train not pass this sign until opposing train reaches switch.*

The ABS signals protecting Winslow Tunnel extended to Schaberg from the north. This explains the meet sign at Schaberg. Schaberg was also mentioned in a number of Frisco employee timetables as where retainers were adjusted on southbound trains after being used to maintain braking down the grade.

382.7 ARMADA – Look for the open pastures and private grade crossing just north of the I-49 bridge. This was a typical small mountain community, with the Nordin/Norden family living here by the 1830s and the Spencer family by the Civil War. The arrival of the Frisco Railroad changed things. Jacob "Jake" Conrad Yates built a series of general stores along the Frisco, including one at Armada. Other stores were built at Mountainburg, Chester, Winslow and West Fork. A post office existed at Armada from 1888 to 1943. For a time, the White River Lumber Company was based here. The 1926 Frisco Official List of Officers, Stations, and Agents listed this location as Walkers, and some documents indicate that the name was changed to Armada in 1928.

In early 2011, the A&M replaced the Riley Creek bridge at this location. The original bridge was built in 1911, and the new bridge is a modern concrete ballast deck span.

383.2 INTERSTATE 49 – High above is Interstate 49, built in the 1990s to connect Fort Smith with booming northwest Arkansas. On January 8, 1999, the road was fully opened to traffic and was designated I-540 and also named the "John Paul Hammerschmidt Highway" in honor of a former U.S. Representative from Arkansas. The state of Arkansas originally asked AASHTO to allow the Interstate segment between Fort Smith and Bentonville to be named Interstate 49, to emphasize plans to extend the route from Shreveport, Louisiana through Arkansas to Kansas City, Missouri. AASHTO refused, and the route opened in 1999 as a northern extension of I-540. However, thanks to the help of the State of Missouri, the roadway north of Interstate 40 at Alma became Interstate 49 in April 2014.

383.9 HOWARD FORK OF FROG BAYOU BRIDGE – Many maps show this stream to be Clear Creek, but the original Frisco maps call it Howard Fork of Frog Bayou.

Route Guide: Springdale to Van Buren

Since that is the name the railroad originally used, this stream will be known as Howard Fork throughout this guide.

Clear Creek/Howard Fork forms on the south side of Winslow, and stays wet around the Washington/Crawford County line and heads south, forming the valley that the rail line follows from Winslow. The railroad crosses the creek several times before the waters enter Frog Bayou. This bridge is 390 feet long and consists of a ballast deck pile trestle, several deck plate girders, and open deck pile trestles, running north to south.

Notice the wider fence lines just to the north of the bridge. Instead of the normal 100-foot wide right-of-way, it is 200 feet wide here. This location was identified as Walkers (milepost 384) in the January 1910 *Official Guide*. The first county maps that shows Walkers as a location dates from 1895. The Walker family owned land nearby.

The longest tangent (straight track) on the railroad starts here heading south, existing for just over three miles. This area also marks the return of homes and businesses as the land levels off and roads are able to penetrate the countryside.

386.1 **CHESTER** – In 1882, the Frisco completed the railroad between Fayetteville and Van Buren, passing a point near Captain James C. Wright's cabin in the valley of Howard's Fork Creek. With activity increasing in the area, Wright built a small store near the tracks in 1883, creating the first business in what would be Chester. A small community quickly grew and it took the name Chester, named for Chester, Iowa, the hometown of one of the locomotive engineers.

The Chester post office opened in 1883 soon after the arrival of the railroad. "CH", or Chester, was once an important terminal on the line. With the steep grades to the north, the Frisco designated Chester as a division point in 1884. A number of helper locomotives were stationed in Chester with the resulting engine facilities (turntable and roundhouse) and yard tracks built by 1887. These helpers were used to assist trains up the grade to Winslow.

In March of 1887, Captain Wright laid out the town of Chester on the east side of the railroad track into nine blocks. From the beginning, the community catered to and thrived because of the Frisco railroad. A two-story station was originally built to provide a home for the local agent, but it burned in 1896. The following year, the division point at Chester was moved to Fort Smith according to the *1897 Frisco Annual Report*, and the population of Chester soon peaked. Because of this, the building that replaced the original station was much smaller, but it soon burned also. Finally, a small four-room wooden depot (40'x24') was built in 1907 on the east side of the tracks. With changes on the line, the roundhouse was removed in the early 1900s. The turntable at Chester was still listed in the 1950 employee timetable (ETT), but was gone in the 1952 ETT, which is when the line was pretty much dieselized. A siding has existed here for years, located at 860 feet above sea level.

For many years, Chester was a shipping point for area lumber and farm products. J. W. Emerson started a sawmill in 1887 to supply lumber and ties. Also operating in Chester were the White River Lumber Company and the Arkansas Lumber Company. Chester was also a shipping point of wild ginseng, which during the 1910s was worth as much as $5 a pound.

Little remains of the early years of Chester. Destructive fires in 1908 and 1936 destroyed all the early frame buildings. The two-story brick building to the east is the only business building still standing from Chester's early years, and is listed on the National Register of Historic Places. Built in 1887 and today known as the Chester House Inn, it was originally known as the Colonel Jacob Yoes Building. The two-story Yoes Building was built to house both a hotel and mercantile store. The entire

Route Guide: Springdale to Van Buren

second floor was devoted to guest rooms. The lower story was divided with the hotel lobby, dining room, and kitchen in the south half and the mercantile store in the north half. Within a few years, a one-story addition was made on the north side of the building to house Butler's Saloon.

A business directory dating from the late 1800s lists several businesses in the town, including mercantile stores, barber shops, a meat market, a sawmill, a blacksmith shop, and three carpenters. Chester also had doctors, drugstores, hotels, and saloons, along with churches and a combination school and Masonic Lodge hall. A population of nearly six hundred people lived in the vicinity of Chester during this time.

387.0 **INTERSTATE 49** – The railroad again passes under Interstate 49. Just north of here at milepost 386.7 is a talking hot box detector. This detector announces its findings on the railroad's radio.

387.1 **HOWARD FORK OF FROG BAYOU BRIDGE** – This bridge is 633 feet long and is located in a curve as the line avoids Rumpus Ridge, located to the south. Just to the south of the ridge is Lake Fort Smith. This bridge has open deck timber spans on each approach and then a series of mixed span types, including deck plate girders and I-beam spans. The mix of span types is due to several flash floods over the years.

387.5 **HOWARD FORK OF FROG BAYOU BRIDGE** – This time the railroad crosses Howard Fork on a 220-foot long bridge made up of deck plate girder spans with timber ballast deck spans on each approach.

388.0 **HOWARD FORK OF FROG BAYOU BRIDGE** – This bridge is 438 feet long, and like other bridges in the area, has timber ballast deck approaches with deck plate girder spans directly over the stream. This stream flows into Frog Bayou just downstream from here.

388.8   FROG BAYOU BRIDGE – This bridge is located at an elevation of 732 feet above sea level. North of here the grade is about 1.2% for more than a mile. The grade levels just south of here for a short distance.

This 537-foot long bridge consists of a number of span types including a through plate girder, a through pin connected truss, I-beam spans, and a series of open deck pile trestle spans. The through truss span has a builder's plate that gives a build date of 1898 but the piers have an inscribed date of 1928. According to the website *Bridge Hunter*, the question is whether this bridge was moved here from another location in 1928, or if the concrete piers were built to upgrade and reuse the bridge that was already here. Nevertheless, a build date of 1898 would make this the oldest truss bridge in Crawford County still open. It is interesting to note that during the 1960s, this bridge was speed and tonnage restricted by the Frisco, the only restricted bridge on the line besides the Arkansas River bridge at Van Buren.

Frog Bayou Bridge at MP 388.8. Photo by Barton Jennings.

Route Guide: Springdale to Van Buren

Frog Bayou forms in Crawford County and flows southwest from Lake Fort Smith through Mountainburg to Rudy and its confluence with the Arkansas River just a few miles northeast of Fort Smith and the Oklahoma State Line. For those who float streams, Frog Bayou is a narrow Class I to II stream. Its primary source of water is Lake Fort Smith and whatever rainfall happens in the area.

Lake Fort Smith serves as the source of municipal water for the Fort Smith area. The lake was recently enlarged to almost 1400 acres, combining it with Lake Shepherd Springs. The new dam measures 190 feet by 3,300 feet and includes the former 89-foot high Lake Fort Smith Dam. Passengers on the train may be able to glimpse the dam at certain times of the year. Lake Fort Smith State Park was rebuilt as a part of the lake's enlargement and features a long list of facilities.

389.2 **GILLIOZ** – Gillioz was listed as having a 10-car spur at one time. Gillioz is an unusual name, but the M. E. Gillioz Company of Monett, Missouri, was a major highway contractor in the area. It is likely that this was a material yard for their use while building roads and bridges in the area during the 1930s.

390.2 **MOUNTAINBURG** – Mountainburg is a small community that first prospered with the coming of the railroad, and then with U.S. Highway 71. The construction of I-49 has hurt the small town as several businesses serving travelers have closed and moved elsewhere.

The railroad arrived here in September 1882, and the depot (built 1892) acquired the telegraph code MB. This two-story depot was a bit unusual in that the entire second floor consisted of living quarters, as opposed to most on the line where the living quarters were only above the office and waiting room. However, the depot was only 50 feet long and 20 feet wide with a smaller freight room. The depot once stood on the west side of the tracks.

A post office located here was first known as Mountainburch (1876-1893), and then Mountainburg (1893-present). Mountainburg is at 712 feet above sea level.

The Narrows is located on the southern slope of a mountain ridge just east of Mountainburg. The site is a small rock shelter or "overhang" roughly 15 feet deep and 30 feet wide. The shelter contains a series of painted petroglyphs consisting mainly of anthropomorphs or "human-like figures." The figures are pecked into the rock surface and some are colored with a black pigment, although on some of the figures red pigment is also used. This combined style of both etching and painting is a unique stylistic variation of what is said to be a combination of Plains Indian and Eastern Woodland traditions. Habitation of the site is associated with the 15th century Fort Coffee phase giving the Narrows rock art an approximate age of 500 years.

While passing through Mountainburg, if you look to the east you might see more old "history" of the area. In the Mountainburg park are three huge recreated dinosaurs: a T-rex, a Brontosaurus, and a Triceratops. All have been here from the early 1980s and two of them – the Brontosaurus and the Triceratops – have an open area where children can climb inside and be in the belly of a dinosaur.

391.1 FROG BAYOU BRIDGE – The 290-foot bridge consists of through plate and deck plate girder spans. It is an often-photographed railfan location. Originally, the highway was to the west and crossed Frog Bayou on what was known as Silver Bridge Road, old Highway 282. With the construction of I-49, a new Highway 282 was built to the east as the first connection back to U.S. Highway 71. The new Highway 282 crosses the railroad at grade at milepost 391.8, just north of Hurricane

Route Guide: Springdale to Van Buren

Creek. The highway will follow the railroad into Van Buren.

391.9 **HURRICANE CREEK BRIDGE** – The railroad crosses this small mountain stream on a 255-foot-long bridge made up of open deck pile trestle and deck plate girder spans. Hurricane Creek forms less than ten miles to the northwest, and flows into Frog Bayou just to the east of this bridge. This area features a number of cattle farms with open pastures and hay fields.

394.3 **INTERSTATE 49** – The railroad again passes under I-49. Look way up to see it! The I-49 bridge also crosses over Frog Bayou and Arkansas Highway 282.

394.7 **FROG BAYOU BRIDGE** – This 343-foot bridge is made up of three deck plate girder and one through pony plate girder spans as well as open deck pile trestle spans on the south approach. Arkansas Highway 282 also passes under this bridge, certainly the most photographed location on the south end of the Arkansas & Missouri Railroad. During the early 1930s, there was a station here named Amrita, also known as Grotto.

The name Amrita has an interesting history. On December 4, 1920, Amrita Grotto was organized with 54 charter members from area Masonic organizations. After several years of using the area for picnics, the group decided to build a country club. On July 4, 1925, the new country club was opened by the Amrita Grotto Masons at a cost of $24,000. There was a large stone lodge and eight cottages, each containing two rooms and a porch. There were also a golf course and zoo. Many visitors used the adjacent railroad to get to Amrita Grotto (a Frisco station was listed here 1927-1933). However, the complex didn't survive the Depression, and it burned down during the early 1930s. Today, all that remains is a pile of rocks.

395.2 FROG BAYOU BRIDGE – This 368-foot bridge is the site of numerous Frisco and A&M publicity shots. It consists of seven through plate and deck plate girder spans. Between this Frog Bayou bridge and the Clear Creek Overflow bridge, the railroad right-of-way is 200 feet wide instead of the normal 100 feet wide.

395.6 CLEAR CREEK OVERFLOW BRIDGE – This bridge is 159 feet long and consists of several deck plate girder spans. The right-of-way varies between 150 feet and 250 feet wide for the next mile south for tracks associated with Lancaster.

395.8 LANCASTER – Located at 616 feet above sea level, Lancaster was at one time a busy shipping point for area farm produce. Reports indicate that the area produced fruits as well as cotton and corn. Lancaster was listed as a station by the Frisco 1886-1942 (other sources say 1882-1947). The post office in Lancaster lasted fewer years, 1882-1933.

The station at Lancaster was very unusual in that there was only one waiting room, and it was located between the office on the south end and the freight room to the north. Built in 1896, it was also an unusual size at 40'x12'. It was located on the east side of the main line where the remains of an old road can still be seen.

William Steward came to Van Buren in 1836 and purchased land from the government upon which Lancaster was built. He built a home in 1837, moved his family to this land and built the first grist mill and saw mill in the county. The town was to be named after Judge Jesse Turner of Van Buren, but Judge Turner asked that it be named after his home town of Lancaster, Pennsylvania.

396.4 FROG BAYOU BRIDGE – This bridge is 521 feet long and is located at 610 feet above sea level. It, like most bridges in these bottoms, consists of a number of deck

Route Guide: Springdale to Van Buren

plate girder spans with open deck timber spans on each approach. Lancaster Road crosses Frog Bayou just to compass-south using a low-water bridge, and then passes under the railroad-north end of the A&M bridge. At this location, a southbound train is actually heading northwest.

Frog Bayou Bridge at Lancaster.

398.2 STEWART – Stewart was named for the Stewart family that farmed this area. There was a spur here for only a few years around 1910. A Frisco station list shows a station here 1905-1917. To find the location of Stewart, look for the open pastures to the east as the railroad rounds a curve just south of the railroad ledge between Frog Bayou and the adjacent hillside. Nothing remains today of Stewart except for a few road traces.

The March 8, 1923, issue of the *Fayetteville Democrat* had an article about Brush Stewart's mysterious death. The article "'Brush' STEWART Found Murdered On Rudy Roadway" stated "His head literally torn from his shoulders by a charge of shot fired at close range striking him squarely in the forehead causing instant death, the body of J. B. "Brush" Stewart, well known

Crawford county farmer residing three miles north of Rudy, was found in the road near his home at noon yesterday. Officers investigating the case declared that they believed robbery was the motive of the slaying. Stewart, according to officers, was known to carry a large sum of money on his person and relatives informed them that he left home at 8 o'clock yesterday morning with $700 in a money belt about his waist beneath his clothing. Stewart was about 54 years of age, it was said, and married, though he and his wife had been separated for about two months. Officers would not make any statement in regard to the matter of clues which they are understood to have obtained but did state that they expect to make arrests in short order."

398.5 **FROG BAYOU BRIDGE** – This bridge is 482 feet long and includes ballast deck timber spans on the north approach and several deck plate girder spans.

399.1 **FROG BAYOU BRIDGE** – This bridge has ballast deck timber spans on the south approach as well as a number of through plate and deck plate girder spans. The total length is 520 feet. South of here, the countryside becomes more open with numerous pastures and a few poultry farms.

401.1 **RUDY** – Rudy was named for local landowner George Rudy. The area was also known as Kenton. A fairly large (68'x20') wooden depot (built 1907) once existed to the east of the tracks toward the business district, using telegraph code RU. A post office opened in 1883 when the railroad came through.

Rudy was a shipping point for area fruits and vegetables, as well as railroad ties and cedar fence posts. Frisco records indicate that the station was closed in 1965.

That is Arkansas Highway 282 at the main grade crossing in Rudy. It bridges over Frog Bayou on one of the few road bridges in the area.

Route Guide: Springdale to Van Buren

401.6 **BALL** – Ball was a short spur track named for former Frisco Assistant Superintendent of Transportation A. M. Ball (1930s).

402.2 **BRIDGE** – This is a short ballast deck timber bridge, only about 112 feet long.

403.6 **MEADOWS** – There was a spur here before World War II, often known as Meadows Switch. Frisco records indicate that Meadows was first recognized as a station in 1901, and it closed in 1947, the same year that a number of other Frisco stations were closed. The rural community of Meadows is located to the east of the tracks about one-half mile. The area has seen a recent housing boom as Interstate 49 passes through the east side of town.

404.0 **FROG BAYOU BRIDGE** – The railroad crosses Frog Bayou for the last time, this time with a bridge 204 feet long using several deck plate girder spans.

404.3 **LILLIE** – Look for the grade crossing with County Road 18, also known as Lost Beach Road. There was a spur here 1883-1898 and the wider railroad grade is easy to spot just north of the grade crossing. A post office operated here between 1887-1898 under the name Zenobia. Later it was called Lillie.

405.8 **FURRY** – The station of Furry existed for a few years before the Depression (1913-1927) just about where the grade crossing with Arkansas Highway 282 exists today. Signs of the old spur track can still be seen north of the grade crossing. Furry, actually located a short distance to the north, was named for P. W. Furry, the railroad agent at Van Buren. Furry is located at the top of a small hill with short approaches of 1% from each direction.

407.2 **FLAT ROCK CREEK BRIDGE** – This bridge is 238 feet long and consists of open deck pile trestles on each approach with a deck plate girder span in the middle. Heading south, the railroad starts entering the suburbs of Van Buren.

407.8 **SMELTZERS** – A 10-car spur existed here before World War I. The station (some sources show a station here 1905-1927) was named after M. F. H. Smeltzer, a local peach grower. The railroad passes under Interstate 40 at Smeltzers.

408.3 <u>COPP</u> – A long siding has been here for years. The siding is often used by the A&M to spot cars for the turn from Springdale or to store cars until they are needed.

409.9 **VAN BUREN RUNAROUND** – Crews use this short siding, located on the east side of the mainline, to runaround their passenger trains.

410.0 **VAN BUREN STATION** – The first Frisco train reached Van Buren on November 15, 1882. This 1902 Victorian-style railroad depot (VN) replaced the original depot, located near the Missouri Pacific mainline. The station may look familiar as is was used for a scene in the film *Biloxi Blues*.

 The Van Buren area was settled by David Boyd and Thomas Martin in the year 1818. After Arkansas became a territory in 1819, Daniel and Thomas Phillips constructed a lumber yard in the community to serve as a fuel depot for river traffic. In the year 1831, a post office was constructed for the community, at the time known as Phillips Landing. This post office was named after the newly appointed Secretary of State, Martin Van Buren.

 Van Buren was first incorporated December 24, 1842. John Drennen along with his partner, David Thompson, purchased the area for $11,000. They moved their business of supplying firewood for steamboats to this new location on higher ground. The courthouse

Route Guide: Springdale to Van Buren

was constructed on a lot of land donated by Drennen on the condition that Van Buren become the county seat. Today, the Crawford County courthouse is the oldest functioning courthouse west of the Mississippi River.

The Rest of the Railroad

Over the years, the Arkansas & Missouri Railroad has operated a number of special passenger train trips over much of the rest of the railroad between Monett and Fort Smith. For those fortunate enough to ride one of these trips, or for those who just want to learn more about the railroad, the railroad territory between Monett (MO) and Springdale (AR), as well as the track south of Van Buren (AR) is described here.

The route north of Springdale passes through the booming Springdale-Rogers metropolitan area, the rugged mountainous country near the Civil War battlefield at Pea Ridge, and the Ozark Plateau area of southwestern Missouri. Passengers here can see the modern Ozarks as well as the more traditional small town hill country.

Van Buren south, the railroad passes through the urban area of Fort Smith, the source of a great deal of freight business for the A&M. The Fort Smith Trolley Museum operates short trolley trips through the streets of the town, and even sponsors a few A&M trips out of their museum grounds. For history buffs, the route also passes through the Fort Smith National Historic Site, the home of the courtroom of Judge Isaac C. Parker, and the Fort Smith National Cemetery.

This route guide includes current as well as former station locations, historic towns, and major stream crossing along the line, listed by milepost. Stations and industrial tracks currently listed in the Arkansas & Missouri Railroad employee timetable are underlined.

Photos by Barton Jennings.

Route Guide: Monett to Springdale

282.0 <u>MONETT</u> – Monett is a town with many names. The location was originally called Billings, but the citizens of the old town petitioned in October, 1871, to have the name changed to Plymouth. In June, 1876, George A. Purdy, agent of the Atlantic & Pacific Railroad Co., petitioned the court to vacate the town plat of Plymouth. At this time the company solely owned the town, so there was no objection to vacating the plat. This allowed the railroad to redesign the town to better fit their plans for building southward into Arkansas.

In the early 1880s, some sources show the name to be Plymouth Junction or Plymouth Crossing. Added confusion comes about because postal sources show the place to be Gonten during the mid-1880s, taken from the name of a local postmaster. However, the confusion was finally settled when in its daily edition of May 2, 1887, the *Pierce City Empire* announced that the railroad had changed the name of the town from Plymouth to Monett. The new name of Monett came from Henry Monett, who was the general passenger agent for the New York Central & Hudson River Railroad.

During the late 1800s, Monett was definitely a railroad town, using the telegraph call letters of "MO". Many of the street names came from active Frisco railroaders. The first YMCA was the "magnificent Railroad YMCA", built in 1898. Later, Monett also had a full-scale Fred Harvey House and Hotel operating at the Frisco Depot, located between 4th and 5th Streets on the north side of the mainline. The Harvey House hotel and dining room was a large complex according to the February 1910 Sanborn map. It was located east of the Frisco station and fronted 5th Street all the way north to Dry Creek. The November 1917 Sanborn map shows no Harvey House, replaced by a "Mail Rm & Coach Rm" building. The 1917 Sanborn map also shows a "R.R. Porters Y.M.C.A." at 506 Bond, two blocks north of the Frisco station. The Frisco Line Harvey Newsstand opened in 1896 and closed in 1930. Some of the foundations of this complex can still be seen on the north side of the BNSF mainline opposite the west end of the railyard.

Many people are confused by a Harvey House on the Frisco. It should be noted that the St. Louis and San Francisco Railroad (the "Frisco") was a part of the Santa Fe Railway until 1897. Harvey began working with the Santa Fe during the early 1890s and the agreement included the Frisco. A number of hotels, restaurants and newsstands were built along the line. Additionally, dining car service on the Frisco was operated by Harvey until 1930, when the railroad decided to buy him out and take over its own food operations.

The Monett railyard was a busy place, being located at the junction of two major Frisco routes to the southwest. The railroad also had a turntable and large roundhouse to serve the many steam locomotives based out of Monett. The roundhouse was located on the south side of the yard just east of the wye. Today, the yard is still busy with trains of the Arkansas & Missouri interchanging with BNSF.

In May 1957, local passenger train #709 would leave Monett at 2:30am with a scheduled arrival in Fort Smith at 7:20am, and leave at 7:55am to go on down to Paris, Texas, arriving at 12:30pm. Northbound, Local Passenger #704 would leave Paris at 1:20pm, arrive at Fort Smith at 5:40pm. After servicing, the train would depart Fort Smith at 6:30pm and arrive at Monett at 10:55pm.

Over the years, Monett developed a number of other industries. These included livestock, apples, tomatoes, a cigar factory, ice plant, razor/cutlery factory, creamery, poultry, dairy and the famous "Ozark" strawberries. Monett became known as the Strawberry Capital of the Midwest. The fruit business was very important in Monett's growth and reportedly the first licensed auctioneer in Missouri operated with the Ozark Fruit Growers Association of Monett.

Route Guide: Monett to Springdale

Monett is in Barry County. The county was organized in 1835 and named after William Taylor Barry from Kentucky, a United States Postmaster General.

282.2 **C.D. JUNCTION** – C.D. Junction is the wye switch in Monett. C.D. stands for Central Division, the territory from Monett south through Fort Smith (AR), Hugo (OK) and Paris (TX), as well as associated branchlines. Located at an elevation of 1,287 feet, C.D. is at the bottom of a hill that reaches all the way to milepost 285. In 1910, Frisco passenger timetables listed St. Louis to Fort Smith as Table #1.

To the west is the Schreiber Foods facility. Schreiber is a dairy company which produces and distributes cheese, processed cheese, cream cheese and yogurt. Reportedly, the company produces cheese slices that are used on cheeseburgers by 17 of the top 20 hamburger chains. The Monett plant dates from the 1970s when the company was growing nationwide. The road that crosses the tracks here is Dairy Street. Just south of here the railroad passes under U.S. Highway 60.

283.0 **SOUTH MONETT** – Look for the Morris Lane grade crossing. This was the line between A&M and BN ownership when the Arkansas & Missouri was created. Heading south, the grade stiffens to 1% upgrade for more than a mile. The A&M uses Track Warrant Control from here south to milepost 339.5. South of here, the railroad passes through a mixture of farm and pasture lands for many miles.

285.0 **WIGHTMAN** – Wightman was named for Frank A. Wightman, the first Republican elected to statewide office in Missouri. A station was located just south of Farm Road 2030, where a patch of woods exists today, from the mid-1910s until the 1970s. A siding once also existed on the east side of the mainline. Apparently, there were once also plans for a station between mileposts 286.1 and 286.6 as the usual 100 foot wide right-of-way is 200 feet wide in this area.

From Wightman to near the Arkansas state line much of the land is used for cattle grazing, dairy operations, poultry farms, and the raising of hay.

287.2 **"GOODNIGHT SAG"** – Nearby is Goodnight Cemetery, thus the name. The Goodnight family lived in this area during the 1800s and a large percentage of the graves here are for the Goodnight family.

The bottom of this sag is at a short timber bridge over Hudson Creek. The railroad comes beside Missouri Highway 37, located just to the west. There are grades of 1% uphill in both directions from this point. Northbound, the grade is only for a mile or so. Southbound, the tracks climb to about milepost 293 on what has been known as "Cyclone Hill."

289.6 **PURDY** – Today a town of about 1,000 residents, a post office opened here in 1880. Known briefly as Winslow during the initial construction of the railroad, Purdy was later renamed for George A. Purdy, Frisco Land Agent. A large (57'x20') three-room wooden depot once existed here, telegraph letters "RD", to serve the community. It was located on the east side of the tracks. Today, a spur track serves several agricultural industries on the west side of the mainline. The spur once served as a full siding, serving the Purdy Fruit Growers Association Berry Shipping Shed and the Farmers Elevator Company. A third track to the east of the mainline once served a number of industries along Front Street.

A Frisco caboose is located in a park about a block east of the tracks. According to the St. Louis-San Francisco (Frisco) Railway Historical and Modeling Society, the caboose is former Frisco 1416, "one of the Frisco built extended or wide vision cabooses intended for local service. The car was constructed in the West Car Shops in Springfield, MO during 9/1975. The car was

Route Guide: Monett to Springdale

constructed with a main car body from former Pullman Standard PS-1 boxcar, SLSF 18469."

Purdy is rather famous in that dancing is not allowed in the Purdy school without permission from the school board. The authority of the school board was upheld in 1990 by the Supreme Court when it refused to hear a challenge by a group of students and parents.

Feed mill at Willow Brook. Photo by Barton Jennings.

293.5 WILLOW BROOK – Once known as Hudson, look for the large grain elevator to the east. As of September 30, 2009, this facility is licensed by the Food & Drug Administration as a medicated feed mill to Cargill Turkey Production. Originally, this facility was built by Hudson Farms, and then was sold to Willow Brook before they sold it to Cargill.

To the west is a new development built for Arkansas & Missouri Railroad's sister company, Ozark Transmodal, Inc. (OTI). Known as the OTI Butterfield Sand Station, this facility is used to transload concrete and mason sand from railcars to a storage area, where it is then loaded into trucks for pickup or delivery. In addition, the facility was also built to provide outdoor storage and transloading capabilities for other commodities, such as lumber and scrap.

294.8 **BUTTERFIELD** – Located at the northern edge of a plateau at 1,536 feet above sea level, Butterfield was platted for investor George Readman, of Edinburgh, Scotland, in 1883. The town was named for Fredrick Butterfield, an officer of the Frisco Railroad Company. About 1914, there was an effort to rename the community Barry City after the county, but the name didn't stick. Today's population is about 400. However, that's not enough to keep a post office, which operated here 1882-1967.

At one time, the Frisco had a small (34'x18') three-room wooden depot (BU) here near 5th Street, along with a packing shed for local farmers. Several photos exist showing Merchants Dispatch refrigerator cars located at the shed.

295.4 **OLD HIGHWAY 37** – The railroad passes under old Highway 37, now County Road 1090.

295.7 **HIGHWAY 37** – The railroad bridges over Missouri Highway 37 here. This road was moved about 1990 to this new alignment. Just south of the bridge and to the west is a new Cargill feed mill. This mill follows the modern design of a loop track large enough for a unit train with a wye at the mainline. This design allows grain trains to come in from either Union Pacific from Van Buren, or BNSF from Monett.

296.7 **COUNTY ROAD 1078/1085** – The railroad again bridges over a county road.

300.6 **EXETER** – The first post office in the area was at El Paso, a few miles west of today's Exeter. Area legend states that Exeter was named by early settlers who settled a short distance west of the present site of the town. These settlers came from Exeter, England, before 1850.

The first plat of Exeter was made for George A. Purdy of the Frisco, and acknowledged by him, on September 29, 1880. The post office moved to Exeter the

Route Guide: Monett to Springdale

same year. Exeter was officially incorporated on February 7, 1881. Plans for the town grew and the first addition to the plat of Exeter was platted by George Parrish, and this plat was acknowledged July 19, 1881, by Green B. Gregory. Gregory made a second addition to Exeter, which was acknowledged October 21, 1883.

At one time there were great plans for Exeter. There was an attempt to move the county seat from Cassville to Exeter and many felt that Exeter would be an important railroad station, being at the top of a series of railroad grades. Exeter, at 1,572 feet above sea level, has the highest elevation of Barry and several surrounding counties in Missouri. However, even with all of these plans, today's population is only about 700.

With the grand plans for the community, the Frisco had a large (72'x20') three-room wooden depot (telegraph EX) here, located to the east of the mainline. The depot was actually a union depot, being also used by the Cassville & Exeter, which had their line on the east side of the building. To the west of the tracks was a stockyard and a strawberry warehouse, and a railroad water tower was located north of the station. A grain elevator once existed north of the stockyards and an apple drying plant was also in the area. A siding of about 6,700 feet existed here to the west of the mainline. The south end of this siding still exists, used as a long storage spur.

As already stated, Exeter was once the junction with the Cassville & Exeter Railroad (1896-1956) which ran 4.8 miles east to the county seat of Cassville. The C&E was at one time an electrified railroad, and in addition, the Cassville & Exeter had a long and somewhat complicated history for such a short railroad. Rails were first installed at Exeter on June 11, 1896, they reached Cassville on June 20th, and the 4.8-mile railroad soon opened as the Cassville and Western Railroad. In 1919, two Cassville businessmen (David Dingler and J. C. Ault) acquired the railroad and made efforts to improve the service. Additionally, with the new owners came a new name, the Cassville & Exeter Railroad.

The little railroad actually had a fair amount of fame. It was featured in the December 12, 1926, issue of *The New York Times*, in 1931 it was featured in *Ripley's Believe it or Not*, and in 1937 it was featured in *Newsweek*. During the 1934 campaign for the U.S. Senate, Harry Truman traveled the railroad. It was also used as the setting for the radio show "Clem & Martha" which aired in the late 1930s – early 1940s. The father of the show's writer was a Presbyterian minister in Cassville who met his wife at the depot where she was a ticket taker.

Both Ault and Dingler died in 1939 and their families fought to keep the Cassville & Exeter Railroad going over the next decade. However, the line continued to deteriorate and the normal 25 minute trip was taking an hour and twenty minutes. In 1947, Ray Dingler became president of the railroad upon his mother's death but closed the railroad in early 1949. Later that spring, Arthur P. Wheelock of Des Moines, Iowa, acquired the railroad and began basic repairs by July. Operations soon began on an as needed basis. However, what little business left soon went away and the railroad closed for good on September 11, 1956.

Downtown, former Burlington Northern Railroad caboose #11619 is displayed on the east side of the tracks. This caboose is an extended vision caboose, originally Frisco #1291, built by Morrison International in August 1969.

303.6 WAYNE – Between 1908 and 1949, Wayne was the junction with the Missouri & North Arkansas (M&NA) line towards Neosho, and eventually Joplin, Missouri. The M&NA operated over the Frisco from here southward to Seligman. Originally called Woodruff, Wayne (telegraph code WN) was the highest station elevation on the M&NA at 1,571 feet. The small 40'x20' three-room depot, built in 1913, was located just north of the junc-

Route Guide: Monett to Springdale

tion with the M&NA. The former depot foundation is to the west of the tracks near County Road 1062. A post office existed here 1913-1955.

303.7 **"WAYNE HILL"** – The railroad crests the grade at 1,580 feet above sea level. Heading south, there is a downward two-mile grade of more than 1%.

306.9 **WASHBURN** – The Frisco served this community with a small (42'x20') three-room wooden depot (WU), built in 1904 and abandoned and ready to fall down by 1960. The depot was located on the east side of the Frisco mainline in line with South Street, two blocks north of the Highway 90 grade crossing. To the west at this location, look for the large white building near the tracks. That is the old tomato canning factory and warehouse. A siding once existed alongside the building for railcar loading. In fact, a 1914 Sanborn map shows that there were three tracks passing through town: an industry track to the west, then a siding, and then the mainline next to the depot. In 1914, the canning factory wasn't where the white building stands today, but instead the Washburn Canning Company was a block north of the northernmost grade crossing at Washburn, along with a set of cattle pens.

The first documented settler was Judge Cureton of Washington County, Arkansas, who moved to the area in 1840 and bought the area where Washburn is now located. When Cureton died in 1853, his property was sold to James T. Keet, who laid out Keetsville and then opened a store there. Keetsville was destroyed in February 1862 as troops fought in an early Civil War battle. After the war, Keetsville was resettled starting in 1867. The next year, a petition was passed to rename the town Washburn, and a post office opened. Washburn, and the surrounding Washburn Prairie, were named in honor of Samuel Washburn, an early settler who reportedly ran a post office in his store.

The railroad was built just west of Washburn in 1879-1880, and the railroad named its station O'Day, after John O'Day, a Springfield-based attorney for the railroad. O'Day and Washburn became sister cities, with the two communities growing together and sharing businesses and citizens. The town of Washburn was officially incorporated on August 4, 1880, while O'Day remained unincorporated. The two communities were basically merged in 1892 when the post office at O'Day was closed and merged with the post office at Washburn. About the same time, a common public school was built to serve both communities. With the merger, many of the old Washburn businesses moved closer to the tracks. The population grew quickly and a number of industries located at Washburn. While the population peaked at about 1,000, today's population is about 450.

The John G. Harbin home, one mile south of Washburn, was the last stage stop in Missouri for the Butterfield Stage Coach mail route before entering Arkansas. Washburn is also located on the historic Trail of Tears and on the Old Wire Road.

312.8   **SELIGMAN** – This area was first known as Herdsville. About 1838, Jacob Roller moved to this area from Scotts County, Virginia. Soon, the village was renamed Roller Ridge in honor of Roller (Roller Ridge Road still serves this purpose). In the winter of 1879 and 1880, the railroad from Monett arrived in the area and the St. Louis & San Francisco Railroad platted a new town here. On September 27, 1880, railroad president, E. F. Winslow donated 80 acres for the purpose of building the town. The town was renamed Seligman in honor of Joseph Seligman. Seligman was an investment banker and founder of J & W Seligman & Company, Inc., now Seligman Investments. (According to the company: "Since 1864, generations of investors have used Seligman® investment solutions to build their wealth. From financing the railroads to developing some of the first mutual funds to pioneering technology investing, the Seligman brand has a reputation for insight, integrity and independent thinking.") The town was incorporated on March 8, 1881.

Seligman, his brother, and a cousin had invested in the railroad industry. Establishing himself as the original "finance capitalist", he insisted on a place on the board of directors of the Atlantic & Pacific Railway (A&P at that time was a franchise of the St. Louis & San Francisco Railway) in order to protect his investment. Through financial manipulations, political payoffs, and synchronization with his European supporters, Joseph Seligman managed to retain control over the A&P for many years. According to *Goodspeed's 1888 History of Barry County*, Joseph Seligman passed away in April of 1881. When the town was named in his honor, his widow, Babette, was so pleased she donated one acre of land and $500 to erect a church house. The local Seligman residents raised another $300, and the Union Church, still standing, was constructed in 1884.

Seligman became the temporary terminal point of the Arkansas Division of the St. Louis & San Francisco Railway upon its arrival. Construction soon restarted and the line reached Fayetteville in 1881. Meanwhile, on June 26, 1880, the Eureka Springs Railway Company was granted a charter to build from the Missouri state line to the resort community of Eureka Springs, Arkansas. On September 21, 1880, a charter was also granted for the Missouri & Arkansas Railroad Company of Missouri to cover the mileage in Missouri. On February 27, 1882, the charters were combined as the Eureka Springs Railway. With this, construction of the line between Seligman and Eureka Springs began later that year and the first train operated over the line on January 24, 1883. Eventually, the railroad was extended under the name of Missouri & North Arkansas all the way to the Mississippi River town of Helena, Arkansas. The M&NA was reorganized as the Missouri & Arkansas and eventually abandoned soon after World War II. The line from here to Harrison, Arkansas, was preserved as the Arkansas & Ozarks in 1950. However, even the A&O failed and was abandoned in 1961.

For the passenger train enthusiast, the M&NA operated one passenger train each way daily. The Joplin to Helena train #201 arrived at Seligman at 9:05am, and then departed at 9:30am. Train #202 would arrive at Seligman at 6:55pm if it was on time, and then depart at 7:10pm.

In 1909, the Frisco depot (SI) was destroyed by fire and rebuilt in 1910 as a frame building measuring 145'x24'. From north to south, the building included a freight room, express room, baggage room, women's waiting room, office, general waiting room, and an open covered porch. The *Cassville Democrat* reported on March 9, 1966, that the Seligman Frisco Station would be destroyed for good. Look for its foundation to the east of the tracks just north of Eureka Avenue.

At one time, there were a number of tracks at Seligman, including a siding to the east of the depot and a long siding to the west of the Frisco mainline. The depot siding was used by the M&NA to reach the station and to interchange freight traffic with the Frisco. The west siding has now been cut back to just a short spur track at its south end.

314.5 **ARKANSAS/MISSOURI STATE LINE** – This is the boundary between Barry County, Missouri, and Benton County, Arkansas. It is just about the center of the curve at this location. The railroad is still on a plateau at 1,570 feet of elevation.

Missouri borders eight different states. No state borders on more. Missouri became the 24th state on August 10, 1821. Today, Missouri is the 21st largest and the 18th most populated of the states. Known as the "Gateway to the West", Missouri was the starting point and the return destination of the Lewis and Clark Expe-

Route Guide: Monett to Springdale

dition, as well as the starting points of the Pony Express Trail and Oregon Trail.

The Territory of **Arkansas** was admitted to the Union as the 25th state on June 15, 1836. It is the 29th largest state, and the 32nd most populated. This part of the state is the Ozark Plateau/Mountains. This is part of the interior highlands region, the only major mountainous region between the Rocky Mountains and the Appalachian Mountains. Arkansas is also the only state where diamonds are mined, and you can go mine them yourself at the Crater of Diamonds State Park.

314.8 GATEWAY – The post office at Gateway opened in 1939. Gateway was a very busy station beginning in 1963 when it opened to bring in materials and equipment for the construction of nearby Beaver Dam on the White River. The station was quiet again after the dam's completion until Ozark Transmodal, Inc. (OTI) built a sand transload facility on the east side of the mainline here. However, after years of growth, demand exceeded the facility's capacity and the new OTI facility north of Butterfield was built. Midwest Walnut (logs) is still located here.

Just south of the transload facility, the railroad crosses U.S. Highway 62 on a concrete span built in 1934, at milepost 315.2. Highway 62 heads east through Eureka Springs and across northern Arkansas. Heading south, today's Highway 62 follows the railroad off to the west, but the original highway (known as Old Highway Road) is located immediately to the east for the next mile.

The name Gateway reflects its location as the gateway into the hills of northwest Arkansas. The terrain changes a great deal here. North of Gateway, the country is gently rolling Ozark plateau – a mix of farms, pasture, and chicken production. South of Gateway, the land becomes much more mountainous until Avoca. East of Gateway is some of the most rugged country in the

Ozark Mountains. If you head west, the plateau country quickly turns into open and drier country.

315.9 OSBORNE – Look for where Old Highway Road crosses the tracks where the railroad comes back to U.S. 62. An 8-track spur once existed here during the 1920s and 1930s. Reportedly, the track was used for shipping railroad ties and other timber products. Osborne was also listed as a passenger train flag stop at about the same time. Records from the time show that there was an Osborne family living in the area.

Other names used for this location include Herd's Switch and Hurd Switch. In 1890 the Post Office Department considered opening a Post Office at this location. The local name for the location was "Switch" but the post office rejected the name, instead naming it "Herd" when the post office opened, named after a local family. Various documents show that the name was spelled "Herd" and "Hurd" by various sides of the family and by locals. Mail was often addressed to "Herd's Switch" or "Herdswitch." The post office closed in 1910 and the post office at Garfield began to serve the community.

316.7 "GARFIELD HILL" – Topping off at 1,635 feet above sea level, this is the top of 1% grades in each direction. For southbound trains, it is a two mile climb to this location from Gateway and then a 2½ mile drop to near Garfield.

317.2 "DEVIL'S EYEBROW" – Long story here, but when surveyors reached here in 1880, "Uncle Arch" Blansett reportedly said "Build a railroad right through these mountains? You can't do it, man, you can't do it. You might as well try to build a railroad on the devil's eyebrow as to undertake to build one in such a place!" As we all know, the railroad was built and this location took the name of Devil's Eyebrow in pride.

Route Guide: Monett to Springdale

This area consists of a number of five degree curves and the line swings along the hillsides. Some great views are also available if you look to the east. In this area is the Devil's Eyebrow Natural Area, a facility of the Arkansas Natural Heritage Commission and the Arkansas Game and Fish Commission. It was formally dedicated in May 2013 during the first recorded May snowfall in Arkansas history. The Natural Area includes the Indian Creek valley, an arm of Beaver Lake. The area has a good population of deer, turkey, and squirrels, and an occasional bear is seen here. It is also a popular roosting area in winter for bald eagles. Devil's Eyebrow is also the only place in Arkansas where the rare black maple tree is found. The tallest mountain in that area is Trimble Mountain with an elevation of 1,720 feet.

319.7 **GARFIELD** – When the St. Louis & San Francisco Railroad built through northwest Arkansas, the company established a station at Garfield (telegraph code JA), west of the existing Pine Log settlement. This was the only level location for a number of miles through this area. The grade heading south again drops at more than 1% to the Little Sugar Creek Bridge at milepost 325. James A. Garfield had recently been elected president and assassinated, thus the name. The post office opened here in 1887.

Mike Condren's website (condrenrails.com) includes a copy of a Frisco Lines "Floor Plans of Station Buildings." It shows that the Garfield depot was built in 1881 as a 32'x18' building with four rooms labeled as "Negro Waiting Room", "White Waiting Room", "Office", and "Freight Room." The station with its gravel platform was on the west (compass north) side of the tracks with the waiting rooms on the railroad south end of the depot.

The Garfield Elementary School is listed on the National Register of Historic Places. The school is the newest of several schools that have stood at this location.

Work on the main building of the Garfield School began in the late 1930s, with funds allotted by the National Youth Administration. The "new" school was completed in 1941.

325.2 LITTLE SUGAR CREEK BRIDGE – We cross Little Sugar Creek on a 288-foot long deck plate girder, one of the scenic highlights of the north end of the railroad. Little Sugar Creek forms in the hills to the east and flows west to where it joins with Big Sugar Creek to form the Elk River near Pineville, Missouri. Elk River then flows west, terminating in Grand Lake O' the Cherokees in Oklahoma.

Notice the short, very steep grade just to the north of the bridge. The grade here is listed as being 2.23%. Heading south, the track again climbs at more than 1% for about two miles. This grade played an important role in the November 29, 1907, train wreck on Little Sugar Creek Bridge. Heading northbound from Avoca, a freight began to run away down the grade. Knowing that a freight train was ahead of it, the engineer of the runaway train began blowing warning signals and the crews of both trains jumped to safety just before the slow train was rear-ended by the runaway. Hitting the slower train on the bridge, the runaway train's engine fell more than forty feet into Little Sugar Creek. Reports state that the only casualties were four show horses and a great deal of whiskey on the leading train. The bodies of the horses were recovered, but there was no sign of any of the whiskey.

325.5 BRIGHTWATER – Brightwater, shown in some Frisco documents as Bestwater, was first settled about 1840 but the station here was gone by about 1905. The town is often spelled Bright Water. A post office existed here 1882-1907.

Just to the north of Brightwater is part of the Pea Ridge National Military Park, which preserves the site of the largest Civil War battle west of the Mississippi River. According to the National Park Service, "On March 7 & 8, 1862, 26,000 soldiers fought here to decide the fate of Missouri. The 4,300-acre park honors those who fought for their way of life. Pea Ridge was one of the most pivotal Civil War battles, and is the most intact Civil War battlefield in the country."

The Pea Ridge battle was also the site of the only formal military use of Indian soldiers in the Civil War. Under the command of Brigadier General Albert J. Pike of the Confederate Army, Indian troops included 1st Cherokee Mounted Rifles, 2nd Cherokee Mounted Rifles, 1st Choctaw and Chickasaw, and 1st Creek Mounted Rifles. The two Cherokee Mounted Rifle units participated in a major assault of Northern cannon positions.

The battlefield area around the tracks includes a number of former Federal defensive trenches. The trenches were here to protect Telegraph Road, which has shaped the history of northwest Arkansas more than any other land feature. It has brought settlers, commerce, prosperity and war to the region. Many parts of the original road still exist and are in use today.

Until the mid-1840s, the road was used primarily by the Army to move supplies and correspondence between Springfield, Missouri and the garrison at Fort Smith, Arkansas. During this period, it was referred to as the Military Road. In 1838, thousands of Cherokee Indians moved along the Military Road near the end of their forced exodus from their ancestral homes in Georgia and the Carolinas. Due to the extreme hardships endured along the way, the route, including the Military Road, became known by the Cherokees as the Trail of Tears.

As the frontier moved west and the threat of Indian attack diminished, the Army reduced its presence in the region. The road, now known as the Springfield to Fayetteville Road, became the region's primary route for commerce with Missouri. Small towns began to develop along the road, including Bentonville, the region's second largest community and the county seat for Benton County. From 1840 to 1860, Benton County's population increased over 300% as the road brought settlers to the region, many of them farmers and hunters from Tennessee.

The Butterfield Overland Stage began running along the road in 1858. Two years later, in 1860, the region's first telegraph line was strung along the road, giving the road its last, and most enduring name – the Telegraph or Wire Road. The telegraph line ran from Springfield, Missouri to Fort Smith, Arkansas, but was cut less than a year later when Arkansas seceded from the Union.

For those who are interested, this area gets its name from the wild peas that grow here. When the first white settlers arrived, the wild peas were very abundant and that is why the area is called Pea Ridge.

327.1 **AVOCA** – Avoca was promised a station by the Frisco in 1881 if a nearby community would relocate to the top of the hill at this location. In 1881, Mr. Peel moved his general store and post office, originally located near Brightwater, about a mile and a half away to where Avoca sits today, thus Avoca was formed. Sources vary about how the name Avoca came about. One source says that Mr. Peel's wife was responsible for giving Avoca its name. She believed "Avoca" was an Indian name meaning "the gathering place." However, other sources say that Albert Peel selected this name after hearing an Irish railroad worker recite lines from a poem by Thomas Moore. "Sweet Vale of Avoca" is part of that poem.

By the 1920s, Avoca businesses using the railroad included stock yards, fruit elevators, and several canneries. The station at Avoca used telegraph code "CA." Mike Condren's station book shows that the original frame station was built in 1908 and was slightly larger than the Garfield station, but with the same basic floor plan. The plan shows that it was on the east side of the

Route Guide: Monett to Springdale

mainline. A siding of 6,727 feet was once located to the west of the mainline. It has been shortened and has generally been used by the A&M for car storage, loading of logs, and the unloading of sand and gravel.

With the construction of nearby Highway 62 and the start of the Depression era setting in, businesses began leaving. It wasn't until the construction of nearby Beaver Lake that Avoca again began to grow. In fact, Avoca was finally incorporated in 1966. Avoca is the north end of a large plateau and the railroad grade simply reflects the rolling nature of the terrain to Springdale. That is U.S. Highway 62 immediately to the west of the tracks.

About two miles south of Avoca at milepost 329, look to the east for a view of the Pepper Source plant. Pepper Source was founded in 1987 in response to the growing need for private label hot sauces in the retail market. At one time, Pepper Source was producing over 100 different labels with 50 warehouses from coast to coast. The original manufacturing facility was located in St. Martinville, Louisiana, and the company was headquartered in New Orleans.

In 1991, the original hot sauce plant was built in Van Buren and began production of one item: Hot Wing Glaze. They soon added a BBQ Sauce, which was to be applied to wings at a processing plant in Berryville, Arkansas. Demand required the company to expand, opening a plant near Rogers in December of 1999. Today, Pepper Source manufactures over 230 products and supplies all of the major poultry companies in the United States.

330.0 TENENBAUM RECYCLING GROUP – TRG opened at this location in 2011 and is a buyer of all ferrous and nonferrous metals such as car bodies, old appliances, aluminum cans, copper, brass, and stainless steel. To the west is the Rogers Municipal Airport, known as Carter Field, with a 6,011' x 100' runway. Until the completion of the new Northwest Arkansas Regional Airport, this was the home of the private air fleet of Walmart and many other regional companies.

332.0 **BENTONVILLE BRANCH SWITCH** – To the west is a 3.5-mile branch line that ends at the edge of Bentonville, Arkansas. The line once saw numerous passenger trains and extended almost fifty miles to Grove, Oklahoma. Today, the line serves a few customers. See the "Route Guide: Bentonville Branch" in the next section for additional information.

332.7 **ROGERS** – The railroad reached Rogers (R) on May 10, 1881. The town was named for C. W. Rogers, Frisco Vice-President and General Manager, who was aboard the business car on the first train to the site. There are a number of side tracks through this area, but still many less than there once were.

The first station at Rogers was built of wood and later included a Harvey House restaurant with a large sign hanging over the platform reading "Frisco Line Lunch Room Fred Harvey." The Frisco station was on the west side of the tracks, with the Harvey House to the south of it. A new brick station was built in 1912, located south of Cherry Street and the former wooden station and the Harvey House. Measuring 144' long and 36' wide, from north to south the station included a Fred Harvey news stand and a women's waiting area against the north wall. Next was a general waiting room measuring 49'x27', with an office and boiler room next. Just to the south of the office was the "Negro Waiting Room" and then a baggage room and express room. There was also once a Fred Harvey Dining Hall as a part of the new station complex. A large concrete platform (approximately 600 feet long) existed on each side of the mainline. The brick station was torn down in 1977.

Rogers was a center of business for the Frisco for many years. During the 1920s, Rogers was the home of Hussey-Hobbs Tie Company. Rogers Milling Com-

Route Guide: Monett to Springdale

pany was also located here, several blocks north of the station at Chestnut Street. Rogers Milling consisted of three large buildings and was the source of the nationally marketed "Rogers Special Patent" brand flour. The Frisco protected this product by providing a special rate to move Kansas wheat to Rogers and the finished flour out to various national markets.

There was once a Frisco TOFC (trailer-on-flat-car) ramp at Rogers to serve local customers, located a block south of the station location. There is some local talk that the ramp was designed to handle Walmart traffic but the railroad wouldn't make the investments that Walmart required. Apparently, the ramps were for single direction only and Walmart wanted ramps for trailers facing both north and south. This issue added one or more days to many of the shipments, shipments that had to be turned on a wye to unload.

In the past, Rogers was served by several railroads and had two roundhouses. The first roundhouse built was a small Frisco structure that was built in 1880 and removed during the late 1880s. The second roundhouse was a three-stall structure built by the Arkansas & Oklahoma Western, a predecessor of the Kansas City & Memphis Railway.

At one time, the Rogers Southwestern Railroad (RSW), later the Arkansas, Oklahoma & Western Railroad (AO&W), and even later the Kansas City & Memphis Railway (KC&M), broke off at Rogers and headed to the southwest. The KC&M developed a network of lines in the area to the west between the Frisco line and the neighboring Kansas City Southern. A line paralleled the Frisco between Rogers and Fayetteville, running about six miles to the west through Hazelwood, Cave Springs, and Tontitown. The original RSW main ran westward between Cave Springs and the KCS at Siloam Springs. Finally, the KC&M later acquired the Monte Ne Railroad and developed a branch from Hazelwood eastward to the resort at Monte Ne, to the east of the Frisco.

The Rogers Southwestern was chartered on February 2, 1904, by the same people who had earlier built the Arkansas & Oklahoma. Construction on the line toward Siloam Springs began during November 1905. To gain access to downtown, Rogers gave the railroad rights up First Street from the south edge of town to Cherry Street and then through the alley between First and Second Street to Elm. With construction faltering about halfway to the KCS, the line was sold to the Arkansas, Oklahoma & Western (known locally as the All Off and Walk) on February 13, 1907. The AO&W had plans to build westward into Indian Territory and also eastward at least as far as Eureka Springs. Construction resumed quickly and the line was opened between Rogers and Siloam Springs on January 1, 1908. To help build eastward, one of the stockholders of the AO&W purchased the Monte Ne (see Monte Ne Junction on the next page) and a connection was finally made after the Frisco removed the old diamond and forced the AO&W to build an underpass.

On December 17, 1910, the Kansas City & Memphis filed for a charter with plans to acquire the local railroads and build a large empire between the cities in the railroad's name. The KC&M bought the AO&W in 1911 and opened a line between Cave Springs and Fayetteville on August 22, 1912. However, the plans to build on across north central Arkansas to Memphis never happened, nor did the planned lines southward to Little Rock and eastward to Eureka Springs and Harrison. However, a large steel bridge was built across the White River east of Monte Ne. Some repots state that some limited service operated east of the river while others state that no rails ever reached the bridge. Things didn't go well and the railroad acquired a receiver on July 18, 1914. When the federal government took control of the most of the nation's railroads during World War I, the KC&M was deemed unnecessary and was abandoned for the rails to pay off the railroad's debt.

Route Guide: Monett to Springdale

336.9 KC&M RAILROAD UNDERPASS – This is the underpass that the Arkansas, Oklahoma & Western /Kansas City & Memphis was forced to build to get to the tracks of the Monte Ne Railroad. See the Rogers write-up on the KC&M for more details.

337.5 MONTE NE JUNCTION – This is the location of the junction (1905-1907) with the original Monte Ne Railroad. The Monte Ne Railroad was built by William Hope "Coin" Harvey, a national figure who campaigned against usury (interest on loans) and for silver coinage. Harvey had a great deal of power nationally, as he had been the campaign manager for the presidential campaign of William Jennings Bryan. Harvey acquired land southeast of Rogers, which he renamed Monte Ne, Spanish for "mountains of water." In late 1900, Harvey incorporated the Monte Ne Investment Company to create a community to restore traditional southern entertainment. With local roads being rough, he also organized a five-mile-long railroad to bring people to the resort. At the resort, Harvey built a number of hotels and cottages, most connected by a series of canals from the train station. The community and railroad were borderline successful, but the Depression and Harvey's death in 1936 ended the project. Today, the community rests beneath the waters of Beaver Lake, visible only during periods of low water levels.

Today, at what was once Mont Ne Junction, the railroad passes through a major truck maintenance facility of J.B. Hunt. J.B. Hunt Transport Services is one of the largest trucking and transportation companies in the United States. The company was incorporated in 1961 and founded by Johnnie Bryan (J.B.) Hunt. Based in Lowell, J.B. Hunt was the first major trucking company to move heavily into the rail intermodal business, initially with the Santa Fe Railroad. Today they have contracts with just about every major railroad in the country, and many intermodal trains run almost exclusively for the company. For J.B. Hunt, the rail business is actually their largest source of revenue and profit, exceeding even their truckload business.

338.0 LOWELL – Lowell started as a small settlement known as Robinson's Cross Roads, settled in the 1840s about a mile east of here along what was later called Old Wire Road. A post office was established there in 1847, though it later closed. As the population grew after the Civil War, the post office reopened under the name of Bloomington. Bloomington became commonly known as "Mudtown", reportedly after a rider for the Butterfield Overland Express got his stagecoach trapped in deep mud there.

When the railroad came through in 1881, it located about a mile west of the town. The residents of Bloomington began contemplating a move closer to the railroad. A tornado in Bloomington helped them make the decision, and the settlement shifted nearer the tracks. The present site of Lowell was owned by J. H. McClure, who donated lots to the Frisco when it built through the area. This community was named Lowell when the post office opened late in 1881.

Lowell is the headquarters location of the nation's largest publicly owned trucking company, J. B. Hunt Transport Services, Inc. Lowell also has the sixth highest median household income in Arkansas, and the highest in northwest Arkansas.

A short siding existed to the west of the mainline. The frame depot built here in 1882 was identical to the one at Garfield and was located on the east side of the main line. Several rail shippers are located here including Advanced Environmental Recycling Technologies (AERT), Lowell Iron & Metal, and Zero Mountain.

For those looking for entertainment, Lowell celebrates Mudtown Days the last weekend of May each year.

Route Guide: Monett to Springdale

340.3 VOGEL – Between the 1910s and the 1930s, a short 4-car spur existed to the west side of the mainline at this location. It was used for handling apples from surrounding orchards. After the spur's abandonment, the cut here was deepened as part of a line improvement program. Today, Arkhola Sand & Gravel has a large facility here.

Just south of here is a community known as Bethel Heights. It is also the location of an October 17, 1897, wreck between two trains. The pileup killed two men, one of them an "unidentified tramp", and five were badly injured. As local news accounts state, the locomotives themselves were reduced to an "unrecognizable mass of wood and iron."

341.4 BENTON COUNTY/WASHINGTON COUNTY LINE – Located in the extreme northwest corner of Arkansas is **Benton County**. The county was created in 1836 from lands in Washington County and was named after Thomas Hart Benton, a prominent U.S. Senator from Missouri. The county seat is at Bentonville. Benton County was the home of Walmart founder Sam Walton, as well as the home of the trucking firm J. B. Hunt. Reportedly, in 1901, Benton County led the nation in apple production, producing 2.5 million bushels of apples and becoming known as the "Land of the Big Red Apple." By 1938, Benton County was the largest broiler-producing county in the nation, fueled by Tyson Foods and Peterson Hatchery.

In 1828, **Washington County** was created and named after George Washington. It was created from lands known as "Lovely's Purchase," comprised of Osage Indian lands purchased in 1816 and given to the Cherokee Indians for settlement a year later. By the late 1820s, white settlers were allowed to settle in Lovely's Purchase. Fayetteville is the county seat and home of the University of Arkansas.

341.9 NORTH YARD – North Yard is the center of freight activity at Springdale. The tracks here are used to assemble and break up the trains to Monett and Fort Smith, as well as support the activities of local switchers. In this area can also be found any A&M locomotives awaiting rebuilding. At times, this fleet looks like a rainbow of historic colors. To the east of the yard is a large Cargill food processing facility.

Between North Yard and Springdale are a number of customers, many on an industrial lead to the east at milepost 342.6. On this industrial lead are such companies as Stock Building Supply, Newly Weds Foods, Kawneer, and Americold Logistics.

343.1 SPRINGDALE – The Frisco gave Springdale the telegraph code "SA". For the Arkansas & Missouri Railroad, Springdale is the center of operations. A new locomotive shops complex east of the tracks maintains the equipment. Just to its south is the headquarters of the railroad, with the new passenger station further to the south across Emma Street. Freight trains operate out of Springdale, both northbound and southbound.

The newer Frisco station was built in 1923 of brick and was 196 feet long and 37 feet wide. It featured the waiting rooms and office on its south end with a very large freight room on the north end. It was located to the west of the main line and was torn down in 1982. It was replaced by a metal building (still used by the A&M) built by the Burlington Northern in 1982. All of the remaining BN agents in northwest Arkansas (Bentonville, Rogers and Springdale) were centralized in this building.

For the history of Springdale, check out the Introduction to Springdale section of this trip guide.

Route Guide: Monett to Springdale

Photo by Sarah Jennings.

Route Guide: Bentonville Branch

The branch to Bentonville has a rather interesting history. During the early 1880s, a few citizens built a crude private railroad between Rogers and Bentonville. During May of 1898, the Arkansas & Oklahoma Railway was chartered with plans to acquire the private road, rebuild it, and extend the line northwestward to Gravette on the Kansas City, Pittsburg & Gulf (later Kansas City Southern). It didn't take long to do as the railroad reached Gravette by fall of that year. The line soon drew the interest of the larger railroad, and the Frisco bought it in November 1900, pushing the line on west into Indian Territory as far as Grove (Oklahoma) in 1909, for a total of just under fifty miles.

For several years (1914-1916), the Arkansas Northwestern interurban, organized and built by the owner of the Park Springs Hotel and Resort at Bentonville, used the line between Rogers and Bentonville. The interurban used a McKeen motorcar to handle the passengers. However, the last interurban train ran on June 11, 1916, when the Frisco ordered service stopped due to lack of payment for the trackage rights. The Rogers to Grove railroad primarily served local farmers, especially the local apple orchards and strawberry fields, but trucks soon took over the business. In 1940, the line west of Bentonville was abandoned. The line into downtown Bentonville was removed by the early 1990s, leaving a 4.6-mile long branch. In 2014, the NorthWest Arkansas Community College bought the end of the line to allow an expansion of the campus, leaving the line less than 3.5 miles long.

B332.0   **MAINLINE SWITCH** – This is known as the Bentonville Branch Switch on the mainline. Just west of here is the grade crossing with North 2nd Street, which is also Highway 62B, at milepost B332.1. Also at this location is the switch to the east leg of the Rogers Wye. The switch for the west leg of the wye is at milepost B332.3. The wye was used to turn freight cars so they could be unloaded from the correct side of the car, a common issue many years ago when railcars were loaded and unloaded by hand.

B332.9 INDUSTRIES – For the next half mile, there are several industries that the railroad serves on the branch. The first is Don's Cold Storage & Transportation, a refrigerated warehouse and transportation company providing blast freezing, cold storage and transportation services to food industry customers in the lower 48 states. DCST also has the only public-access rail head in Rogers. They operate more than 2.5 million square feet of cold storage, conduct container loading and rail transloading.

Just west (MP B333.0) is Superior Spray Systems, a leader in manufacturing high quality spray foam rigs and equipment for commercial and residential applications. Next at milepost B333.5, at what once was known as Irelan, is the Glad Manufacturing facility.

B334.4 BEAVER LAKE CONCRETE – There is a short siding to the north for unloading sand, gravel, and other materials. Beaver Lake Concrete is owned by the Monarch Cement Company, before 1913 known as Monarch Portland Cement Company (founded 1908), based in Humboldt, Kansas.

Just west of Beaver Lake Concrete at milepost B334.7 is a spur to the south to serve Bekaert Corporation and a plastics facility.

B334.9 APPLE SPUR – There was once a 7-car-length track here. We are near West Hudson Street, also known as U.S. Highway 62. West of here is a spur to the south (MP 335.2) into the Ridout Lumber and Home Center complex.

B335.4 WATER TOWER ROAD – To the southwest is the NorthWest Arkansas Community College, one of

Route Guide: Bentonville Branch

the largest and fastest growing schools in Arkansas. On Friday, January 24, 2014, NorthWest Arkansas Community College voted to buy and remove the Bentonville Branch from this point west. Acquired for $2.5 million, the strip of land about 50 feet wide and 1¼ miles long runs through the campus.

B338   **BENTONVILLE** – Bentonville is the site of the former Frisco stucco station, built in 1925. Listed on the National Register of Historic Places, today the station is used by the Bentonville/Bella Vista Chamber of Commerce. Displayed next to the Bentonville Frisco Depot is fake Frisco Caboose #2841. It is really a Rock Island Caboose.

      Settlers lived in the Bentonville area as early as 1830, but the town was originally known as Osage. The post office was established in December, 1836. The town was renamed Bentonville (some sources say on July 10, 1841, while others say on January 3, 1843) after prominent Missouri Senator Thomas Hart Benton, who had been a strong supporter of Arkansas statehood. The town of Bentonville was selected as the county seat of Benton County upon Arkansas' acceptance as a state on June 15th, 1836. The town site itself was not laid out and platted until November 7th, 1837. In January, 1873, Bentonville was officially incorporated as an Arkansas town.

      Bentonville is still the county seat of Benton County, and the headquarters of Walmart Stores and The Whistler Group, a major U.S. manufacturer of radar detectors. Bentonville is also home to the first Walmart store. On the square in Bentonville is Walton's Five and Ten Cent Store. Today it's the Walmart Visitors' Center, a museum dedicated half to the Walton family and half to the history of the retail chain.

      How did Walmart start here? Sam and Helen Walton lived in Newport in northeast Arkansas where they leased a Ben Franklin discount store franchise. By the end of the term of the lease, they had turned the franchise into the most profitable Ben Franklin store in the nation. The owner of the franchise decided to take over the business and the Waltons suddenly had no business. Looking around, Sam Walton found a store in Bentonville and started again. He soon added stores in nearby communities, using family and friends to operate and invest in them. As is said, the rest is history.

Bentonville Depot. Photo by Barton Jennings.

Route Guide: Van Buren to South Fort Smith

410.0   VAN BUREN STATION – The first Frisco train reached Van Buren on November 15, 1882. This 1902 Victorian-style railroad depot (VN) replaced the original depot, located near the Missouri Pacific mainline. The station may look familiar as is was used for a scene in the film *Biloxi Blues*.

The Van Buren area was settled by David Boyd and Thomas Martin in the year 1818. After Arkansas became a territory in 1819, Daniel and Thomas Phillips constructed a lumber yard in the community to serve as a fuel depot for river traffic. In the year 1831, a post office was constructed for the community, at the time known as Phillips Landing. This post office was named after the newly appointed Secretary of State, Martin Van Buren.

Van Buren was first incorporated December 24, 1842. John Drennen along with his partner, David Thompson, purchased the area for $11,000. They moved their business of supplying firewood for steamboats to this new location on higher ground. The courthouse was constructed on a lot of land donated by Drennen on the condition that Van Buren become the county seat. Today, the Crawford County courthouse is the oldest functioning courthouse west of the Mississippi River.

410.1   7TH STREET BRIDGE – Located at 432 feet above sea level, this steel stringer bridge crosses 7th Street on a 1% downward grade toward the Arkansas River. The railroad is running on the hillside behind the Van Buren historic business district on Main Street.

410.4   VAN BUREN – This is the location of the original Frisco Van Buren station, near the UP Crossing. The location of the station was moved northward as Van Buren's business district developed just above the parts of town that had flooding problems.

410.5 **UNION PACIFIC DIAMOND** – The Frisco once crossed the Missouri Pacific at this location. Today, it is the Arkansas & Missouri crossing Union Pacific (UP).

The track arrangements here have changed over the years. After the Corps of Engineers moved the Missouri Pacific trains to the Frisco bridge, a connection for westbound MP trains was built on the north side of their tracks that connected with the Frisco route southbound just north of the diamond. The old grade is still visible.

Today, a new connection has been built on the south side of the UP mainline so that traffic from the UP yard can head south onto the A&M bridge without tying up the UP mainline. This route also gives the A&M a connection to the Van Buren riverfront to connect to sand barges. Additionally, a connection was built to the northwest that allows UP grain trains from the west to connect directly with the A&M mainline. All of this construction indicates the changes from the early days of the A&M when there seemed to be almost a war between the two railroads. Today, traffic from the UP is a major part of the A&M's business.

The Frisco line was signaled between milepoles 410-21 and 411 by ABS. This signal system was designed to protect trains at the MP Diamond in Van Buren and on the Arkansas River bridge.

410.6 **ARKANSAS RIVER BRIDGE** – At 1,460 miles long, the Arkansas River is the longest tributary in the Mississippi-Missouri River system. From its source near Leadville, Colorado, the river drops 10,000 feet in 125 miles, travels through Kansas, then through northeastern Oklahoma. There, it is joined by the Canadian, Cimarron, Neosho-Grand, and Verdigris rivers. It then crosses Arkansas, emptying into the Mississippi River 600 miles north of New Orleans, Louisiana.

Route Guide: Van Buren to South Fort Smith

The railroad crosses from Crawford County into Sebastian County while crossing the Arkansas River. **Sebastian County** was created in 1851 and named after William K. Sebastian, a judge for the U.S. Circuit Court. The county seat was first located at Greenwood, then moved to the second-largest community in Arkansas, Fort Smith, before being relocated back to Greenwood in 1852. In 1861, it was decided that the county would have two seats of government: one at Fort Smith and the other at Greenwood.

The Arkansas River was a major challenge for the growing Frisco Railroad. In November 1882, the St. Louis & San Francisco Railway Company arrived in Van Buren and regular service between Monett and Fort Smith began in January 1883. To cross the river, the railroad used the Little Rock & Ft. Smith's transfer boat *Harold B* (a double ended side wheeler) until 1886.

Several sources provide a very detailed history of the Frisco bridge over the Arkansas River. Congress authorized the Frisco railroad bridge at Van Buren on July 3, 1882. However, the authorization was subject to approval of the company's plans by the Chief of Engineers, United States Army. The railroad's plans were submitted on November 6, 1882, but were rejected on November 24. After more than a year of arguments, the Frisco agreed to a number of changes and received permission to build the bridge on January 26, 1884.

In 1885, the Union Bridge Company began to build a wrought iron and steel bridge (1,794,247 pounds of iron and 1,153,191 pounds of steel) to cross the river. Construction was first slowed by high water during 1885 and then by a shortage of iron. The original bridge rested on 10 piers numbered from the Van Buren bank southward. The piers were made of white limestone, mainly from a quarry near Beaver, Arkansas (on the M&NA line to Eureka Springs), with lesser amounts coming from quarries in Mountainburg and Garfield. The construction of this bridge, technically owned by the Frisco's Fort Smith & Van Buren Bridge Company subsidiary, took two lives. The first train to cross the bridge was southbound Frisco No. 17, on February 9, 1886.

The bridge superstructure consisted of 4 fixed spans of 165' length on the south end and 3 fixed spans of 256'-9" length, separated by a pivot span of 366' length, on the north end. Total length of the original bridge was 1,798 feet. The pivot span, which rotated to allow river navigation traffic when necessary, rested on a circular 30-foot diameter rock pier and rotated on a 27-foot diameter cast and wrought-iron turntable.

The St Louis, Iron Mountain & Southern once had trackage rights over the Fort Smith & Van Buren Bridge Company from the SLSF north connection (29 feet north of SLSF crossing at Van Buren) to the SLSF south connection, located between the Arkansas River bridge and Fort Smith. The total trackage rights mileage was 1.39 miles. The agreement lasted from November 24, 1885 to November 2, 1891.

Due to heavier locomotives and railcars, the Frisco announced plans in 1912 to rebuild the bridge. The plans included replacing the metal superstructure of the original Van Buren bridge with new trusses which were over twice as heavy, to handle axle loads which had also doubled by that time. As the rebuilding was underway in December 1913, high water caused a collapse of the false work used to support the bridge.

Numerous other problems occurred as the Frisco attempted to rebuild the bridge. Local newspapers had dubbed the new bridge the "Jonah Bridge." Although much of the preliminary work had been at least partially finished, a large amount of money had been spent and the bridge now had a large gap in it over the deepest part of the river channel. Additionally, the railroad's only 106 ton derrick had gone swimming in the river along with its three-man crew. The Frisco had to detour via the MP

Route Guide: Van Buren to South Fort Smith

to Sallisaw (OK) to enter Fort Smith for more than a month.

On January 1, 1914, the reconstruction of the bridge was turned over to the Kansas City Bridge Company. By January 11, trains were again using the bridge although it was many months before everything was completed. On April 7, 1914 newspapers announced that the steel work was finally finished. The bridge project was formally finished April 27, 1915.

In May 1943, major flooding again took out several spans of the bridge, closing it for several months. During the repairs, a 300-foot through truss span and a 50-foot through plate girder span were added to the south end and 4 deck girder spans were used to replace the lost Span 1 on the north end.

The McClellan-Kerr Arkansas River Navigation System navigation project resulted in the removal of the nearby Iron Mountain (Missouri Pacific) bridge. The Missouri Pacific then returned to using the Frisco bridge from Van Buren to reach Fort Smith. As part of the McClellan-Kerr Arkansas River Navigation System, a new vertical lift span was installed in 1976 in the location of the new channel. This required removal of three of the old spans and replacement by the lift span and a short span.

411.7 **GERBER PRODUCTS SPUR** – A spur to the west serves the Gerber Products Company. Gerber controls more than 80% of the baby food market in the United States. The *1926 Frisco Official List of Officers, Stations, and Agents* called this area Oak Park (1905-1952). The neighborhood is still known by that name.

The Frisco broke Fort Smith into four different districts for switching assignments. This was District 100. Both the Frisco and Missouri Pacific competed for the manufacturing and warehouse business in this area, most of which located here post-WWII. The two railroads have parallel lines through this area, lines that were essentially used as paired tracks for passing trains. Businesses in the area included a Harding Glass plant (automotive glass), Dixie Cup, and Gerber Foods, as well as a number of team tracks and several manufacturers of packaging for the local furniture industry.

411.9 MISSOURI PACIFIC PARIS BRANCH SWITCH – After the McClellan-Kerr Arkansas River Navigation System project, the Missouri Pacific (MP) bridge into Fort Smith was abandoned and MP acquired trackage rights to use the Frisco bridge. This is where the Missouri Pacific entered their own trackage in the Fort Smith area, located just to the west of the Frisco. At one time, the tracks followed the Frisco through town and then turned eastward to reach a large feed mill at Paris, Arkansas. However, the line was leased to the Fort Smith Railroad in 1991 and eventually the line was abandoned between Fort Chaffee and Paris after the feed mill closed and moved to near Russellville, Arkansas. However, there is still a great deal of local rail business in the Fort Smith area and tracks wind around each other, often with several railroads serving each customer.

The junction here between the Frisco and Missouri Pacific actually existed many years earlier. When the Frisco originally opened their Arkansas River bridge, the MP gained rights into Fort Smith over the Frisco, and a junction was built here for the MP to get back onto their own tracks. Originally known as SLIM&S Junction, it later became known as MoP Junction.

To the east is the large Georgia Pacific Dixie Products pulpboard plant.

412.1 NORTH FORT SMITH – This is a short spur to the east of the main line.

413.8 HILL – From 1905 until 1917, the Frisco timetable showed a station named Hill here.

Route Guide: Van Buren to South Fort Smith

414.1 **F.S.R. DIAMOND** – This location was known as FSSRR Crossing in Frisco Central Division ETT #28 dated May 17, 1936. The name comes from the name of the original builder of the line. Much of the industrial trackage in Fort Smith was constructed by the Fort Smith Suburban Railway Company in an attempt by Jay Gould to keep other railroads out of Fort Smith. It formed a loop around the city. It was later merged into the Missouri Pacific Lines. The crossing was gate protected with the gate lined against the FSSRR.

The crossing has gone through a number of names. About 1967, it took on the name of MoP Crossing, then just M.P. in 1971, then U.P. in 1987, and finally F.S.R. in 1994, when the Fort Smith Railroad leased much of the area's Union Pacific tracks.

414.9 **FORT SMITH NORTH YARD** – To the east of the mainline is a five-track yard, as well as a transload and warehouse facility. This was once the main terminal on the Frisco between Springfield (MO) and Texas. The yard handled classification for local switching, the turn to Springdale/Fayetteville, and freight interchange with the Missouri Pacific, Kansas City Southern, and Rock Island. Through trains sometimes changed power due to the ruling grade to the north. On November 13, 1922, the railroad closed bids for a 300-ton concrete coaling station at Fort Smith. The contract for the coaling station was awarded to Roberts & Schaefer Company of Chicago. The roundhouse was demolished soon after steam ended on the line, but engine service facilities and company stores were still active almost to the date of the A&M's founding. The old Frisco turntable, built in 1910 by the Philadelphia Turntable Company, was also removed and sold to the Eureka Springs & North Arkansas Railroad. Today, the A&M uses North Yard to build northbound trains and to support local switching.

Photos from the 1920s often show a half dozen or more steam locomotives sitting at the roundhouse.

Documents from the Interstate Commerce Commission's Bureau of Valuation, dated September 27, 1915, indicate that the roundhouse had 15 stalls, with 14 having inspection pits. The size of the roundhouse was due to the number of branches to the south to serve the coal fields in the area, as well as to fight the grades to the north. Locomotives photos from the time show 2-8-0s in the 1300 series, 2-8-2s in the 4000 series, and an assortment of 4-6-0s, 2-10-0s, and a few 0-6-0s. During the early diesel days, power included Alco FAs, assorted Baldwins, standard EMD power, as well as the stray Davenport.

The SLSF yard and downtown businesses north of the depot and Garrison Avenue bridge made up District 200. There was team track activity and a variety of older businesses to the south of the yard. The tracks of the Frisco and MP crossed each other a number of times as they served the area industries.

At the south end of the yard are Wildcat Minerals and Santrol, both sand facilities for drilling. The facilities keep expanding and now hold 25 and 45 railcars respectively. Ozark Transmodal, a subsidiary of the A&M, also has a facility here, as do several other customers. The Ozark Transmodal facility provides a wide range of transloading services for various types of commodities for customers who do not have direct access to rail or need storage of inventory. The Fort Smith facility includes seven acres of outside inventory space and 40,000 square feet of warehouse space. Additionally, the Fort Smith warehouse features a plastics logistics operation which includes packaging and blending capabilities, the only such facility in the region.

415.4 GARRISON AVENUE – This location was in the Central Division ETT #28 dated May 17, 1936. It was the switch into the Frisco passenger station. The Frisco freighthouse was in this area at 111 North C Street.

Route Guide: Van Buren to South Fort Smith

Just north of the Garrison Avenue overpass, look for the Fort Smith Visitor's Center to the west. The Victorian mansion that it is in once housed a brothel, Miss Laura's, restored by the local historical society. Miss Laura's was the first bordello listed on the National Register of Historic Places. Of the seven houses on "The Row" in 1900, Miss Laura's is the only survivor and has served as Fort Smith's official Visitor Center since 1992. Go check out the photos from the building's history and see if you recognize anyone (yes, it has happened)!

A&M 44S at Garrison Ave. Photo by Barton Jennings.

415.5 FORT SMITH FRISCO STATION – This is the site of the old Frisco passenger station, located just south of the U.S. Highway 64 overpass. It is listed on the National Register of Historic Places. The station (FS) was built 1902-1904 by Anderson & Company, of St Louis. The *Railroad Gazette* (August 5, 1904) stated that "the new station at Fort Smith, Ark., is the most imposing of any of the new structures. It replaces an old wooden station and it is situated a block further west at the corner of Garrison Avenue." Architects will tell you that the station was built in the Greek style. There used to be tall

Ionic columns supporting the portico on the north side of the building, but they were removed in the mid-20th century to make room for the bridge to be widened. The building material, limestone blocks cut smoothly to resemble grey marble, were quarried in Carthage, Missouri. The main waiting room was "a spacious 26 feet by 36 feet 3 inches. The interior of the building was finished with hard pine and cypress rubbed with oil." The last through train to serve the Frisco station was Frisco train #709, heading south for Paris, Texas, on January 31, 1958. Dispatchers and supervisory officials had offices on the second floor. There was also a Frisco Line Harvey Newsstand in the building. Currently, the Frisco Station is part of the Fort Smith National Historic Site.

Fort Smith Frisco Station. Photo by Sarah Jennings.

The Iron Mountain brick station was just to the west across the tracks. For information on the railroads in the Fort Smith area, check out Mike Condren's Fort Smith railroad website (condrenrails.com). For those interested, here is a list of the station locations for the seven railroads that served Fort Smith in 1930.

24 Garrison Avenue	Arkansas Central; Fort Smith, Subiaco & Eastern; and Missouri Pacific

Route Guide: Van Buren to South Fort Smith

404 Parker Avenue   Midland Valley

700-10 Rogers Avenue   Kansas City Southern and St. Louis–San Francisco Railway

1000 Garrison Avenue   Fort Smith & Western

    Here are a few more pieces of information about the passenger stations in Fort Smith, a small city with a large number of stations. While the above list of station locations is for 1930, it doesn't include all of the stations in Fort Smith. For example, the Frisco Station at First and Garrison is not listed. The Frisco Station was built in 1903 and used until 1911, when the Frisco began to use the new Kansas City Southern Station, also known as Union Depot, which opened in 1911. The Frisco moved back into their own station in 1948, where they remained until passenger service ended in 1965. The Union Depot was torn down in 1966, replaced by the Fort Smith Civic Auditorium.

    The confusion brought on by all of the train stations led to a 1917 proposal by the president of the City National Bank to build a union station for all of the railroads. This four-track station would actually have connected the Frisco Station and the Missouri Pacific Station by sitting on the south side of the Garrison Street bridge. However, nothing ever happened with the idea except for a great deal of talk.

    Frisco District 300 includes the tracks south of the Garrison Avenue bridge. At one time there were a number of manufacturing facilities in this area. Today, there are a few remaining furniture factories from the days when Fort Smith was a leading producer of home and business furnishings. Much of this area was cleared a few years ago when a tornado hit Fort Smith.

    Also in this area, to the west of the Frisco lines, is a small yard formerly operated by Missouri Pacific. Today, the Fort Smith Railroad uses it as a base of operations. Also in this area are the remains of the former KCS line to the west. Kansas City Southern formerly had its own bridge over the Poteau River, but now uses trackage rights on the A&M/Frisco to reach its small yard and customers. The primary KCS customer in this area is the OK Foods feed mill.

415.6 GARLAND AVENUE JUNCTION – This location was clearly identified in the Central Division ETT #28 dated May 17, 1936. Garland Avenue Junction, or GA Junction, is where the Frisco left its mainline to travel to Fort Smith Union Station, built by Kansas City Southern at 700-10 Rogers Avenue. The connecting track was used by Frisco passenger trains until they switched back to their own station at the foot of Garrison Avenue. The KCS used this connecting track to reach industrial trackage off the Frisco on the north side of town.

Today, this is the site of the South 3rd Street grade crossing. Much of this area has been cleared and is undergoing rebuilding after a severe tornado a few years ago. However, this is the center of a number of historic locations in Fort Smith. Just north of the road crossing is the Fort Smith National Historic Site, the location of the second U.S. Army Fort Smith and the home of Judge Parker and his court. Just south of the road crossing is the Fort Smith Trolley Museum and the Fort Smith National Cemetery.

Fort Smith, as can be imagined, has an early military history. The first Fort Smith was established at the confluence of the Arkansas and Poteau Rivers in 1817 at a place called Belle Point. It was the highest navigable point on the Arkansas River at the time the site was chosen by the U.S. Army. Soldiers arrived in 1817 and named the site Fort Smith after their commanding officer, Thomas A. Smith. The army abandoned the fort in 1824. Foundations from this original construction are visible to visitors today.

Route Guide: Van Buren to South Fort Smith

A second fort was built here in 1838, located a bit higher above the rivers. Major buildings included two officer's quarters, a barracks, commissary, and quartermaster storehouse, all enclosed by a stone wall. The former military barracks and the Commissary Storehouse, the oldest building still standing in Fort Smith, are part of the Fort Smith National Historic Site. General Zachary Taylor, later President Taylor, lived here 1846-1848 while he was Commander of the Western Military District. Remains of his home still exist.

For many people, the name Fort Smith might sound familiar. For anyone who has seen the movies, or read the book, Fort Smith is the base of action for the story of *True Grit*. It was here at the court of Judge Parker that Mattie Ross first heard of, and saw, Rooster Cogburn. While much of the story is fiction, Fort Smith was a base of the legal system for this area and into Indian Territory, now Oklahoma. While Rooster Cogburn wasn't real, there are enough stories about the real marshalls to fill many books. One of the most famous was Bass Reeves, an African-American U.S. marshal who worked under Judge Parker out of Fort Smith. He often rode into Indian Territory with his friend, an Indian policeman. Some have alleged that stories about Reeves could have been the inspiration for the Lone Ranger stories.

In 1872, the former military barracks were converted into the federal courthouse. When the military barracks was used as a courthouse the basement was turned into a jail. In 1888 a new jail wing was constructed. The federal courthouse, which originally was a 1½ story structure with full porches, was changed to its present appearance in 1890.

From 1873 through 1896, eighty-six men were executed on the gallows at Fort Smith. All the men executed were convicted of rape or murder. After the Civil War, there was a mandatory federal death sentence in cases of rape or murder. Of the eighty-six men executed here, seventy-nine were sentenced to death by Judge

Parker. During Judge Parker's twenty-one year tenure, a total of 160 death sentences were handed down. Of that number, 43 were commuted to life in prison or lesser terms; 2 were pardoned by the President; 31 had appeals that resulted in acquittals or convictions overturned; 2 were granted new trials and discharged; 1 was shot and killed while attempting to escape; and 2 died in jail while awaiting execution. During his years on the bench, Parker handled more than 13,000 cases with more than 9,000 of the defendants being convicted or pleading guilty. A reproduction of the 1886 gallows stands on its original site and is a reminder of "the chaotic social conditions that existed in Indian Territory during Judge Parker's time."

The federal court for the Western District of Arkansas still exists today, holding court in the Judge Isaac C. Parker Federal Building, three blocks from the National Historic Site. Today the court has federal jurisdiction over the western counties of the State of Arkansas. The Indian Territory jurisdiction of the court came to an end on September 1, 1896, thus ending the unique nature of the court.

To the east of the railroad is the Fort Smith Trolley Museum, operated by the Fort Smith Streetcar Restoration Association. The Museum operates a short trolley line using former Fort Smith Light & Traction #224, a double-ended single truck, arched roof Birney car, built by American in April 1926. #224 was once used as the "Streetcar Café" in Ashdown, Arkansas, before being restored. The Museum's collection includes a number of other trolley cars from the area, as well as a number of railroad freight and passenger cars, and Frisco #4003 (2-8-2) steam engine.

416.1   MP JUNCTION – This was Midland Valley Junction in Central Division ETT #28 dated May 17, 1936.

Route Guide: Van Buren to South Fort Smith

Fort Smith Trolley Museum. Photo by Sarah Jennings.

416.4 FORT SMITH UNION STATION – Listed in the Central Division ETT #28 dated May 17, 1936, this station was actually on the KCS line.

416.7 KANSAS CITY SOUTHERN CROSSING – The crossing was gate protected, lined against the KCS.

416.9 MP CROSSING/KCS CROSSING – This location was clearly identified in the Central Division ETT #28 dated May 17, 1936. This is where the Frisco crossed the Missouri Pacific Paris Branch.

The Paris Branch, today operated by the Fort Smith Railroad, was originally part of the St. Louis, Iron Mountain & Southern's line to Greenwood. About four miles south of Fort Smith, a line headed east, chartered by the Arkansas Central to build from Fort Smith to Paris, Arkansas. The idea of the railroad was to serve the coal fields in the area. The line was completed to Paris in 1900 after Jay Gould acquired the line.

On July 7, 1991, the Fort Smith Railroad Company, a wholly-owned subsidiary of Pioneer Railcorp, entered into a twenty-year lease with Union Pacific Railroad to operate the line. After a few years, the east end of the line was abandoned after the Tyson feed mill at Paris was moved to the UP mainline near Russellville, Arkansas. Today, the Fort Smith Railroad operates 18 miles of track from Fort Smith to Barling, Arkansas.

417.0 **SF JUNCTION/UNION PACIFIC DIAMOND** – According to Mike Condren (condrenrails.com), SF Junction is where the Frisco, Missouri Pacific, and Kansas City Southern crossed. Northbound Frisco passenger trains using Union Station left Frisco trackage here to return to their own track at GA Junction. A gate located on the MP diamond was normally against the Missouri Pacific.

417.1 **KANSAS CITY SOUTHERN DIAMOND** – The KCS reaches Fort Smith on their own Fort Smith Branch from Poteau (27.7 miles total), the former Frisco mainline south of town. The last few miles into town (KCS mileposts 0.0 to 6.4) are via the A&M.

KCS ETT #5, dated July 19, 2002, states **"FORT SMITH OPERATION VIA THE A&M RAILWAY: From A&M MP 422.5 to A&M MP 417.0, Track Warrant Control is in effect. Trains must secure track warrants and track bulletins from the A&M Dispatcher. Yard limits are in effect between A&M MP 412.0 and A&M 417.0."**

417.2 **MILL CREEK BRIDGE** – This bridge is a 75-foot ballast deck frame trestle. The Mill Creek area was once considered as a separate community. The point where Mill Creek flows into the Poteau River is cited in a survey of the western boundary of Arkansas. For many years, ice was cut from the Poteau River near the mouth

Route Guide: Van Buren to South Fort Smith

of Mill Creek. A native stone ice house was once located just west of the tracks.

418.0   **WARD** – Identified in Central Division ETT #28, dated May 17, 1936, as a two-car length spur track. During the early 1980s, there was still a short spur to the west at this location.

419.1   **RUGE** – Ruge was listed in Central Division ETT #33 dated June 11, 1944. It was still listed as a small spur track in the early 1960s. Several industrial tracks were still here in the 1980s, as well as several spur tracks to the west.

420.4   **FENN** – A large 113-car yard was here from 1936 through the 1960s. A few tracks still existed to the east in the early 1980s.

420.5   **FORT SMITH INDUSTRIAL PARK** – Back in passenger days, the Frisco 7am switch job would take the passenger equipment to the wye at the Frisco Industrial Park in south Fort Smith to turn the passenger train. The main business that the Frisco served in this area was a Whirlpool appliance plant. Originally a Norge facility, the plant has been expanded several times and now features an adjacent warehouse. A small yard, still known as Norge Yard, assists the crews working this major customer.

421.0   **BASHE** – Bashe station was listed in the Central Division ETT #28, dated May 17, 1936. In this area, the former Frisco line bends west into Oklahoma to avoid an east-west ridge that is an outlier of the Ouachita Mountains.

421.1   **ARKANSAS/OKLAHOMA STATE LINE** – The railroad crosses the border between Sebastian County, Arkansas, and Le Flore County, Oklahoma. **LeFlore**

County was created at statehood (1907) from the major part of Recording District 14 in the old Choctaw nation. The name LeFlore comes from Greenwood Leflore, a Choctaw chief and a signer of the Treaty of 1830, in which the Choctaw Indians sold all their lands east of the Mississippi River. Interestingly enough, after the sale, many Choctaws migrated to present day Oklahoma, but Leflore stayed in Mississippi and became a politician and wealthy planter.

422.5 SOUTH FORT SMITH – South of this location to Poteau, Oklahoma, the former Frisco line is now owned and operated by Kansas City Southern. KCS officially leased this trackage from BN on February 9, 1985, then bought it on November 13, 1989.

Glossary

AAR – Association of American Railroads
AASHTO – The American Association of State Highway Transportation Officials
A&M – Arkansas & Missouri Railroad
A&P – Atlantic & Pacific Railway
ABS – Automatic Block Signaling
AERT – Advanced Environmental Recycling Technologies
Alco – American Locomotive Company
AO&W – Arkansas, Oklahoma & Western Railroad
AR – Arkansas
BBQ – Barbeque
BC Rail – British Columbia Railway
BM&E – Black Mountain & Eastern
BN – Burlington Northern
BNSF – BNSF Railway (created by the merger of Burlington Northern and Santa Fe)
CAT – Caterpillar Inc.
C&E – Cassville & Exeter Railroad
CC&E – Combs, Cass & Eastern
EMD – Electro-Motive Diesel
ETT – employee timetable
Frisco – The St. Louis and San Francisco Railway Co.
FSSRR – Fort Smith Suburban Railway Company
KC&M – Kansas City & Memphis Railway
KCS – Kansas City Southern
LIRR – Long Island Railroad
M&NA – Missouri & North Arkansas
MJRX – M. Ryan Railway Service Contractors
MLW – Montral Locomotive Works
MP – Missouri Pacific Railroad <u>or</u> Milepost
MO – Missouri
MoP – Missouri Pacific Railroad
O&CC – Ozark & Cherokee Central
OTI – Ozark Transmodal, Inc.

RSW – Rogers Southwestern Railroad
SLIM&S – St. Louis Iron Mountain & Southern Railway
SL-SF – The St. Louis and San Francisco Railway Co.
SLSF – The St. Louis and San Francisco Railway Co.
SP – Southern Pacific Railroad
StL&SF – St. Louis and San Francisco Railway Co.
TEBU – Tractive Effort Booster Unit (slug locomotive)
TOFC – trailer-on-flat-car
TRG – Tenenbaum Recycling Group
TX – Texas
UP – Union Pacific Railroad
VLIX – vintage locomotive
WCRC – Washington Central Railroad Company
YMCA – Young Men's Christian Association

About the Author and Book

For almost three decades, Barton Jennings has been organizing charter passenger trains and writing the route description, both for planning purposes and for the enjoyment of the passengers. These trips have been from coast to coast, often covering operations that haven't seen a passenger train in decades. In addition, he has written a number of articles about various railroads for rail hobby magazines. In 2014, Bart coordinated the convention of the National Railway Historical Society, which included three days of charter trains over the Arkansas & Missouri Railroad, and wrote the convention guide book. This wasn't the first time he had chartered a train on the railroad, having ridden his first Arkansas & Missouri passenger train in 1988 and having chartered several A&M trains over the years for photography and friends.

Bart was born in northwest Arkansas and still has strong ties to the area. He has been fortunate to get to know many of those who have known and researched the railroad. His basement has several rooms full of books, timetables and other documents about this and other railroads – important research items from a time long before today's Internet. Today, Bart Jennings, after years working in the railroad industry, is a professor of supply chain management and teaches transportation operations. He also still teaches regulatory issues for the railroad industry, a way to stay in touch with the industry he loves.

This book is an outgrowth of all of these experiences and previous writings about the Arkansas & Missouri. Much of the information comes from internal railroad records, government and public records, railroad workers, and conversations with old and new friends. It is hoped that you enjoy your adventure with the Arkansas & Missouri Railroad and that this book is of assistance in some ways – Arkansas & Missouri Railroad: History Through the Miles.

Image courtesy of the Arkansas & Missouri Railroad.

For information about riding one of the Arkansas & Missouri Railroad's passenger trains, call **479-725-4017** or order tickets on their website at **www.amrailroad.com/excursions**.

www.ingramcontent.com/pod-product-compliance
Lightning Source LLC
Chambersburg PA
CBHW050557300426
44112CB00013B/1956